COUNTERING TRUTH DECAY A RAND Initiative to Restore the Role of Facts and Analysis in Public Life

EXPLORING MEDIA LITERACY EDUCATION AS A TOOL FOR MITIGATING TRUTH DECAY

ALICE HUGUET | JENNIFER KAVANAGH
GARRETT BAKER | MARJORY S. BLUMENTHAL

RAND CORPORATION

For more information on this publication, visit www.rand.org/t/RR3050

Library of Congress Cataloging-in-Publication Data is available for this publication.
ISBN: 978-1-9774-0257-8

Published by the RAND Corporation, Santa Monica, Calif.

Cover design by Pete Soriano.

Preface

Media literacy education offers a potential tool to curb Truth Decay, defined as the diminishing role that facts, data, and analysis play in today's political and civil discourse. In this report, we use interviews with experts, a review of existing literature, and an investigation of available outcome measures to better understand key issues in the field of media literacy and to explore the ways in which media literacy education might counter the trends of Truth Decay. We provide recommendations for researchers, policymakers, practitioners, and the wider public.

This report is one of a series focused on the topic of Truth Decay. The original report, *Truth Decay: An Initial Exploration of the Diminishing Role of Facts and Analysis in American Public Life*, by Jennifer Kavanagh and Michael D. Rich, was published in January 2018 and laid out a research agenda for studying and developing solutions to the Truth Decay challenge.

RAND Ventures

The RAND Corporation is a research organization that develops solutions to public policy challenges to help make communities throughout the world safer and more secure, healthier and more prosperous. RAND is nonprofit, nonpartisan, and committed to the public interest.

RAND Ventures is a vehicle for investing in policy solutions. Philanthropic contributions support our ability to take the long view, tackle tough and often-controversial topics, and share our findings in innovative and compelling ways. RAND's research findings and recommendations are based on data and evidence, and therefore do not necessarily reflect the policy preferences or interests of its clients, donors, or supporters. For more information about RAND Ventures, please visit www.rand.org/giving/ventures.

Contents

Figure and Tables

Figure

Tables

Summary

In 2016, researchers at the RAND Corporation began exploring what is now referred to as Truth Decay—the diminishing role that facts, data, and analysis play in our political and civil discourse.[1] The rise of Truth Decay has been brought on, at least in part, by an increasingly complex and saturated information ecosystem. Navigating this environment to complete even simple tasks requires many skills, such as the ability to evaluate sources, synthesize multiple accounts into coherent understanding of an issue, understand the context of communications, and responsibly create and share information. The gap between these demands and the skills of the average individual results in unfortunate consequences, such as a susceptibility to disinformation, misinformation, and bias.

Scholars, educators, and policymakers responding to concerns about disinformation and other symptoms of Truth Decay have begun to consider how educational programs—both in schools and outside them—can help people become more discerning about the content that they consume, create, and share through various media platforms. The phrase *media literacy* (ML) is one way to describe this set of com-

[1] *Truth Decay* is defined as comprising four trends: an increasing disagreement about objective facts and analytical interpretations of data; a blurring of the line between fact and opinion; an increasing relative volume, and resulting influence, of opinion compared with fact; and declining trust in key sources of information that used to be viewed as sources of factual information, such as the government and the media. Jennifer Kavanagh and Michael D. Rich, *Truth Decay: An Initial Exploration of the Diminishing Role of Facts and Analysis in American Public Life*, Santa Monica, Calif.: RAND Corporation, RR-2314-RC, 2018.

petencies.[2] Recent attention to the challenges posed by the complex information ecosystem has increased interest in ML for stakeholders with a variety of interests. This report seeks to inform efforts to apply ML education as a countermeasure to the spread of Truth Decay by drawing on a broad body of knowledge. We are guided by the following questions:

- How is ML conceptualized by experts and in extant empirical literature?
- To what extent does research demonstrate that ML education can build participant resilience to the spread of misinformation and disinformation? What limitations are there to our knowledge of ML effectiveness?
- What publicly available ML resources are currently offered, particularly as applicable to Truth Decay?

We answer these questions with several different types of analyses. First, we use expert interviews to provide a map of ML and related fields, discussing central issues and tensions. Second, we review existing literature on ML interventions, highlighting key insights and identifying limitations. Third, we discuss how ML outcomes are currently defined and measured in research. Finally, we describe a set of publicly available ML resources—in this case specifically focused on news and information literacy—providing descriptive data about program characteristics and focal topics.

Defining Media Literacy

At its core, ML is made up of several specific competencies, such as the abilities to access, analyze, evaluate, and communicate media messages in a variety of forms.[3] Experts and organizations typically define ML

---

[2] By *media*, we refer to information provided formally or informally through print, broadcast, online, mobile, video, and other digital platforms.

[3] Patricia Aufderheide, *Media Literacy: A Report of the National Leadership Conference on Media Literacy*, Washington, D.C.: Aspen Institute, 1993, pp. 9–10.

using these or similar collections of competencies, which in the past two decades have evolved to focus more on the active construction of media and participation in the information ecosystem. Central to ML is the notion that all media are constructed for a purpose and contain embedded biases or filters. ML education teaches participants to consider the implications of message construction from numerous angles, such as how the motivations of those disseminating information could influence content selection and framing and how different kinds of media and other technologies affect the nature of communication.

Within this broadly defined field, there are many related and overlapping subfields, each with different foci and theoretical traditions: information literacy, news literacy, digital literacy, science literacy, visual literacy, critical media literacy, and others. As noted previously, we come to ML with a particular interest in understanding the role that it can play in reducing susceptibility to and the spread of misinformation and disinformation, using Truth Decay as our framework. Some examples of ML competencies relevant to this specific application are the abilities to identify and access information needed to inform decisions and behaviors; evaluate the reliability and credibility of authors, sources, and information presented in varied forms and mediums; assess the processes used to create an informational product; synthesize information from multiple sources; and create and/or share media in a manner reflective of its credibility, with awareness of potential consequences. These competencies correspond most closely with fields of news and information literacy—disciplines at the intersection of civics, journalism, and library sciences—and do not include the full set of broader skills related to ML. Although this narrower set of competencies is at the core of our interest and motivation to explore ML, in portions of this report we widen the aperture of our analysis so that we can extract lessons from the broader ML field.

Insights from Expert Interviews

To gain a better understanding of the key debates, stakeholders, best practices, and open questions in the fields of ML and related literacies, we conducted interviews with 12 experts and used this material to identify key issues and insights that could anchor our understanding of ML and guide our continuing analysis. We summarize key findings here.

Defining ML. Most interviewees agreed that ML has a broad remit, covering the study of all forms of media, including how media messages are constructed, interpreted, and disseminated. We learned from interviewees that news and digital literacy are increasingly important pieces of ML, but the ML field itself is much broader, and a growing focus on these narrower subfields could neglect other important aspects of ML.

Balancing critical thinking and trust. Interviewees emphasized a tension in balancing analytical questioning and skepticism with an interest in establishing and maintaining some level of trust in credible institutions. The danger is that the analytic questioning that is core to ML could be taught or learned in a way that crosses the boundary into cynicism, damaging trust even in credible sources of information. Experts in our sample believed this problem to be avoidable.

Modes of instruction. Interviewees characterized two basic approaches to ML education. With a stand-alone approach, ML is taught in its own course and focused on exclusively. With an integrated approach, ML programming and activities are blended into other content areas in school settings. An integrated approach offers more exposure to ML instruction and a model for how students could apply ML skills in different contexts, but it does have drawbacks. For example, when ML is integrated throughout a curriculum, especially if teaching ML falls to more than one educator, it could unintentionally slip through the cracks. Research does not definitively point to one approach as preferable to the other.

The question of context. To be successful, ML education needs to be responsive to participants' needs, backgrounds, and experiences, particularly in terms of the contexts in which ML is taught, the examples used, and the medium through which competencies are demonstrated and practiced. Experts emphasized that the most effective ML strategies are those that reach participants in a format and context with which they are familiar and comfortable.

Scaling ML education. We heard from interviewees that a central challenge in the field of ML is the need for scale—that is, the ability to reach a much wider audience. Interviewees were not overly optimistic about the prospects for achieving scale in the near term, citing a lack of institutional support and resources. One interviewee said that achieving scale would require reconceptualizing ML education as something that happens in spaces of everyday life.

Assessment. Interviewees generally agreed that assessment and evaluation in the field of ML remain underdeveloped, but they also pointed to areas in which progress is being made. One reason assessment can be a challenge in the ML field is the complexity of competencies involved.

Reviewing ML Literature

With insights from our interviews as a foundation, we conducted a literature review on outcomes of ML intervention. We considered research from numerous disciplines featuring varied methodological approaches and different contexts. We surveyed this literature with two goals in mind: (1) to better understand ways that ML is conceptualized across the field, and (2) to determine the extent to which current studies demonstrate that ML education can improve participants' ML competencies, particularly as related to Truth Decay.

Conceptualizations of ML

Our first question was how existing literature conceptualizes ML. Although research commonly defines ML as the ability to access, analyze, evaluate, and communicate,[4] studies also frame ML in more nuanced ways, particularly for the purpose of developing outcome measures. Reviewing these studies, we identified three primary, but not mutually exclusive, ways that the research tends to frame ML. First, some research discusses ML in relation to the influence of economic drivers on the construction of media messages. Second, a subset of literature focuses on

---

[4] Aufderheide, 1993.

the role of ML in civic life and democracy. Finally, another set of studies focuses on ML as a means to determine quality of information.

Dimensions and Effects of ML Interventions

Taking a broad view, past research suggests that ML education might improve participants' related competencies and skills, but there remains uncertainty in this body of research, and there are several limitations. There is little causal, evaluative research in the ML field that isolates the effects of ML interventions. Furthermore, the studies we reviewed varied widely in how they defined and measured ML competencies. As a result, we are not confident in drawing definitive conclusions from past research, such as what kinds of ML practices work and under what conditions. Still, it is useful to summarize the research that does exist and what we can learn from it. Table S.1 summarizes key research findings, organized by ML intervention characteristic. Each of these findings requires further research.

Table S.1
Summary of Dimensions and Effects of ML Interventions

Characteristic	Summary of Findings
Duration	• Longer ML interventions might be associated with larger effects. • Even brief interventions can improve student outcomes.
Agents (facilitators)	• Evidence is mixed. Some studies find that the identity, skills, and teaching style of the agent are associated with participant outcomes; others find no relationship.
Format	• Although various formats (or the means through which ML interventions are delivered to participants) have been studied, the majority appear to be "traditional" teacher-to-student delivery. • We did not find comparative evidence regarding what formats are most effective in ML interventions.
Participant profiles	• Most studies focus on students in kindergarten through 12th grade or in college. • Less research considers ML for young children, older adults, and marginalized communities.
Creation	• Using some form of media creation in ML interventions appears to encourage positive student outcomes and perceptions of ML.

Measurement and ML

Because ML outcomes and measures are distinctively different from study to study, aggregating findings across studies is a challenge. Aggregated evidence is important in identifying overall patterns of what works and what does not. There are three factors that we identify as contributing to the variation in ML outcomes and measures used across ML and related research. First, ML competencies themselves are nuanced and context specific, making them a challenge to measure. Second, the ways that researchers conceptualize ML competencies is uneven across the literature. Finally, ML research comes from a variety of different disciplines, each bringing its own approach to the research. To be clear, there is value in having a diverse set of measures—if those measures evaluate the same underlying constructs. But having some commonality is also useful for comparisons across studies and over time. Table S.2 lists the variety of measures we identified in the literature. Each measure has advantages and disadvantages. For example,

Table S.2
Types of ML Measures

Type of Measure	Description
Self-report	Allows respondents to rate or judge their own abilities
Multiple choice	Prompts participants to select discrete answers to questions through selection of predesignated answer options
Task-based	Provides students with a set of tasks to complete; scores performance using a rubric or scoring protocol
Computer-based	Uses electronic platform and often employs an adaptive format, adjusting the level of difficulty based on test-takers' responses as the assessment progresses; can feature scenario-based tasks
Portfolio assessment	Collects artifacts related to the learning process, such as reflections on and actual products of the research process, that are then evaluated
Observation	Observes and assesses how individuals interact with media in real life
Online data collection	Observes and assesses how individuals interact with digital media by monitoring online behavior, often at a large scale

self-report measures are low-cost to collect, but they are riddled with problems of bias and cannot capture actual growth in competencies. Multiple choice and computer-based assessments can also be low-cost and easy to score, but they often cannot realistically respond to context because response options are predesignated. Task-based assessments add some realism and context to ML evaluations by asking students to complete a set of undertakings that can mimic real-life scenarios, but they are more costly and difficult to score reliably. Portfolio assessment captures a full body of work collected by a student over time and allows for an evaluation of complex, process-oriented skills associated with ML, but it can be costly to compile and evaluate in a consistent way and is more difficult to scale as a result. Observational data collection (gathered by observing individuals interacting with information) can provide a more nuanced and context relevant assessment of behavior, but this approach is also time-consuming and costly. Collection of large-scale data about online behaviors provides an insightful view into broad patterns in how society interacts with the information ecosystem, but this approach is not designed to evaluate individuals' process-oriented competencies.

An Inventory of Available News and Information Literacy Resources

We were also interested in exploring what ML resources are available to the public. We compiled a list of ML programs, curricula, and other resources that the public can access online. This is not a review of literature, and we do not have any information about the effectiveness of these resources; it is a collection of 50 different resources focused explicitly on news and information literacy topics. This database is intended to provide a centralized location for information about such resources and give interested stakeholders a means for comparing programs across many dimensions. We included ML resources that met our criteria: any resource aimed at news or information literacy topics, available publicly online, and either originating in or being marketed to the U.S. context. However, there are certainly resources relevant to different applications that we did not include. We describe characteristics of these resources, such as program format, target audience, duration, cost, developer, and program content.

Our review highlights the diversity of currently available programs, particularly of their formats and delivery methods but also, to some extent, their audiences. Although some resources feature a full curriculum, others are made up of modules, lesson plans, videos, and activities of varying lengths. Existing resources in the news and information literacy arena tend to focus on students in kindergarten through 12th grade, especially middle and high schoolers, and to some extent on college and university students. There are some resources aimed at educators, a smaller number created for journalists, and others for parents. The most common topics are evaluating source credibility; verifying and checking of facts; creating and sharing media; navigating and accessing information; and separating fact and opinion. Again, we do not have evidence for the effectiveness of these programs and do not recommend any one over another; we offer the inventory as a place for interested parties to begin exploring options for ML education in their own homes, classrooms, or organizations.

Media Literacy Moving Forward

Recommendations for Researchers

Strengthen interdisciplinary communication and collaboration. Our overarching recommendation to researchers in ML is to increase interdisciplinary communication and collaboration. Collaboration could advance the broader field of ML by facilitating information-sharing and joint research efforts among researchers with overlapping or complementary research interests. Synthesizing varied stakeholder perspectives could provide increased depth to studies of ML, given that researchers from different fields bring with them their own sets of expertise. Increased interdisciplinary communication and collaboration also offers an opportunity to raise awareness of ML outside the research community. With a variety of expertise across ML-related disciplines working toward a common purpose, the level of recognition that ML could garner could be beneficial to the field and to the public—particularly at a time when policymakers, educators, and the public are seeking solutions to Truth Decay–related problems. Several mechanisms could serve this objective, such as the development of a regular convening or interdisciplinary forum for discussion, negotiation, and identification of joint needs. Another approach would be to fund interdepartmental fellowships for ML researchers that would allow researchers in one field to work in another. Foundations also might have a role here because they could prioritize these types of exchanges, or interdisciplinary research proposals, creating incentives for researchers to seek diversity in their research partners.

There are any number of possible topics on which an interdisciplinary commission could begin work, but we identify two as prime candidates. *First, we suggest creating a set of shared ML competencies and measures that are relevant and applicable across ML subfields.* This would require exploring the overlap in the ways that ML competencies are defined and measured across ML and closely related fields. To be clear, we do not suggest that all subfields of ML drop their unique competencies or decide on using only a singular form of measure. Identifying where there are commonalities, however, could ground research in this discipline. A set of well-defined competencies could serve as the basis for research and practice in such fields as news literacy, information literacy, and digital literacy, while each would also maintain unique competencies in addition to the common set. Throughout this report, we note the challenges inherent to assessing ML competencies; this interdisciplinary work could be useful for developing a set of measures that capture ML's complex competencies, drawing on different kinds of expertise. This task is ideally suited to a commission made up of experts in various ML-related fields. The work of the commission need not be the final word but could represent a first large step forward and serve as the foundation for future work. This process could strengthen relationships among the varied factions of ML and, importantly, would allow future research from divergent strands of ML to build on each other.

A second potential focus for the interdisciplinary commission could be identifying fieldwide data needs and establishing the platforms to col-

lect that data consistently over the longer term. The field would benefit from acquiring systematic information about the state of ML across the United States. Establishing a platform at the national level for longitudinal data on ML would not only provide a valuable resource to educators, researchers, and practitioners, it could also raise awareness about ML more generally. Surveys could be used to better understand ML in schools and in the general public; for example, a survey to educators could ask questions about the resources allocated to ML, educators' perceptions of their preparation, and additional supports they feel they need. This type of information could guide future research efforts and ultimately lead to recommendations for policymakers and school administrators.

Recommendations for Policymakers, Practitioners, and the Public

Consider the full range of ML competencies. One clear observation that emerged from our analysis is that the ML field pulls from a nuanced body of knowledge, one that was in development well before recent increases in attention to the issues of misinformation and disinformation. As a result, we recommend that practitioners and policymakers turning to ML as a response to these challenges consider not only the narrow aspects of ML that appear immediately relevant (e.g., fact-checking, searching online) but also the full body of evidence that exists about the relationships between individuals and the information ecosystem. Increasing the lines of communication between practitioners and researchers can contribute to this work.

Engage diverse constituencies in scaling ML education. The scaling of ML efforts is both necessary and difficult. One way to scale ML efforts, it seems, might be to use other agents of ML in addition to teachers, and other forums for ML in addition to schools. This might mean enlisting community members—pastors or rabbis, librarians, parents, or professional mentors can serve as agents of ML in both formal and informal ways. Although we need more research on what works when it comes to improving ML, pursuing this decentralized approach to ML education might be one way to achieve the "herd immunity" that the experts we interviewed pointed toward. We note that although this recommendation is aimed first at policymakers and practitioners, *it is also a recommendation with important implications for the general public.* If scaling ML relies on the grassroots efforts of individuals, then parents, coaches, bosses, mentors, and friends could play an important and central role in expanding the reach and success of ML education.

Acknowledgments

We are appreciative of all the support we received during the completion of this report. We thank Michael Rich for his guidance, interest, and feedback. We are especially appreciative of the experts in this field who helped build our understanding of ML. We thank Fatih Unlu for guiding this document through RAND's Research Quality Assurance Process and providing valuable feedback. We also thank our colleagues Jody Larkin, Sohaela Amiri, Stephani Wrabel, and Hilary Smith for research assistance, and Laura Hamilton for her guidance throughout. We are also grateful to our two external reviewers for their comments and insights that undoubtedly improved the report.

CHAPTER ONE

Introduction

In 2016, researchers at the RAND Corporation began exploring what is now referred to as Truth Decay—the diminishing role that facts, data, and analysis play in our political and civil discourse.[1] The rise of Truth Decay is in part attributable to our increasingly complex and saturated information ecosystem. Technology, in particular, offers continuous access to information of varying quality and credibility, information that can blur the line between fact-based evidence and opinion. Effectively navigating the current information environment requires many skills, such as the ability to evaluate sources, understand the context of communications, and responsibly create and share information. It is not clear that the average student emerges from kindergarten-through-12th-grade (K–12) schooling competent in these skills or that most adults—who were educated before the rise of the internet and social media—are any better prepared. The gap between the demands of our information environment and the skills of the average individual results in unfortunate consequences, such as a susceptibility to misinformation, disinformation, and bias. Education, specifically media-focused education, offers one approach to closing the gap between the

---

[1] *Truth Decay* is defined as comprising four trends: an increasing disagreement about objective facts and analytical interpretations of data; a blurring of the line between fact and opinion; an increasing relative volume, and resulting influence, of opinion compared with fact; and declining trust in key sources of information that used to be viewed as sources of factual information, such as the government and the media. Jennifer Kavanagh and Michael D. Rich, *Truth Decay: An Initial Exploration of the Diminishing Role of Facts and Analysis in American Public Life*, Santa Monica, Calif.: RAND Corporation, RR-2324-RC, 2018.

requirements of the information ecosystem and the skill sets that individuals need to navigate it.[2]

Scholars, educators, and policymakers responding to "fake news" and other symptoms of Truth Decay have begun to consider how educational programs, in schools and outside of them, can help people become more savvy about the information they consume, create, and share through various media platforms.[3] The phrase *media literacy* (ML) is one way to describe such competencies. Recent attention to the threat posed by online disinformation to the integrity of elections, federal responses to disasters, and national security has significantly raised the profile of ML for stakeholders with a variety of interests. This report seeks to explore ML and its applicability as a countermeasure to the spread of Truth Decay. We are guided by the following questions:

- How is ML conceptualized by experts and in extant empirical literature?
- To what extent does research demonstrate that ML education can build participant resilience to the spread of misinformation and disinformation? What limitations are there to our knowledge of ML effectiveness?
- What publicly available ML resources are currently offered, particularly as applicable to Truth Decay?

We answer these questions with several different types of analyses. First, we use expert interviews to discuss central issues and tensions in ML and related fields. Second, we review extant literature on ML interventions, drawing out key insights and identifying limitations. Finally, we describe a set of publicly available ML resources—specifically, those focused on news and information literacy—and provide descriptive data

---

[2] By *media*, we refer to information provided formally or informally through print, broadcast, online, mobile, video, and other digital platforms.

[3] As an example of two of the many publications focused on the connection between media literacy and changes in the media ecosystem, see Tricia Tongco, "How People Can Combat Fake News," ATTN.com, December 2, 2016; and Monica Bulger and Patrick Davison, *The Promises, Challenges, and Futures of Media Literacy*, New York: Data and Society Research Institute, February 21, 2018.

about their characteristics and focal topics. In the remainder of this chapter, we define ML and discuss the link between ML education and Truth Decay.

Media Literacy Defined

ML can be thought of as an approach to processing information that can be applied in any context. At its core, ML refers to the abilities to access, analyze, evaluate, and communicate various media messages in a variety of forms.[4] ML experts and organizations typically define ML using these or similar collections of competencies, which in the past two decades have evolved to focus more on competencies related to participation and creation. For instance, the Media Education Lab at the University of Rhode Island defines ML as the ability to "access, analyze, compose, reflect, and take action."[5] Similarly, the National Association for Media Literacy Education frames ML as the ability to "access, analyze, evaluate, create, reflect, and act."[6] Relevant to these competencies, a central concept in ML is that all media are constructed for a purpose and thus inherently come with some degree of bias or filter. ML education also considers how different kinds of media and other technologies affect the nature of communication.[7]

ML is a broad term that connects a variety of interrelated literacies. Within the field of ML, there are many related and overlapping subfields, each with a different focus and theoretical tradition. Librarians, for instance, tend to focus on *information literacy*, or the ability to

---

[4] Patricia Aufderheide, *Media Literacy: A Report of the National Leadership Conference on Media Literacy*, Washington, D.C.: Aspen Institute, 1993, pp. 9–10.

[5] Media Education Lab at the University of Rhode Island, "Key Ideas from Digital and Media Literacy: Connecting Culture and Classroom," webpage, undated-c.

[6] National Association for Media Literacy Education, "Media Literacy Defined," webpage, undated.

[7] Pioneering media scholar Marshall McLuhan famously wrote that the "medium is the message," calling attention to the interaction of medium and content. See discussion in Tessa Jolls and Carolyn Wilson, "The Core Concepts: Fundamental to Media Literacy Yesterday, Today and Tomorrow," *Journal of Media Literacy Education*, Vol. 6, No. 2, 2014.

"recognize when information is needed" and "to locate, evaluate, and use effectively the needed information."[8] Schools of journalism attend primarily to *news literacy*, with an emphasis on consuming, interpreting, and publishing news based on knowledge of accepted journalistic standards. Those involved with *critical media literacy* employ an approach informed by social justice, using ML competencies to identify implicit and explicit biases and oppression in media messages. In addition to these, ML can also be linked with digital literacy (specific to online spaces), visual literacy (focused on graphics and images), science literacy (focused on analytical concepts), and other intersecting literacies. We take the approach that each of these forms of literacy lives under the "big tent" of ML and use the term broadly.[9]

Bounding Media Literacy for This Report

As noted, our particular interest is in understanding the role that ML can play in reducing susceptibility and contributions to the spread of Truth Decay. There is not consensus across the field regarding what specific competencies ML encompasses, but some that we find relevant to our framing include the abilities to

- identify and access information needed to inform decisions and behaviors
- evaluate the reliability and credibility of authors, sources, and information presented in varied forms and mediums
- assess the processes used to create an informational product (e.g., were rigorous journalistic standards upheld? Were accepted research processes employed?)
- synthesize information from multiple sources

---

[8] American Library Association's Presidential Committee on Information Literacy, *Presidential Committee on Information Literacy: Final Report*, Washington, D.C., 1989.

[9] Michael RobbGrieco and Renee Hobbs, *A Field Guide to Media Literacy Education in the United States*, Kingston, R.I.: Media Education Lab at the University of Rhode Island, 2013.

- create and/or share media in a manner reflective of its credibility, with awareness of potential consequences.[10]

This particular set of competencies is at the core of our interest in ML. These competencies correspond most closely with the fields of news and information literacy—literacies at the intersection of journalism, library sciences, and civics—but also overlap with other media-related literacies. This list represents a portion of skills that fall under the umbrella of ML and is only a sample of the types of complex competencies that ML can include. For this report, we interviewed experts from fields related to ML and reviewed studies that framed ML competencies in ways that differed from our own; we focused on literature that addressed ML as tied to a wide variety of topics, such as health, violence, and advertising. Only in our inventory of publicly available ML resources did we narrow the scope to focus on news and information literacy. We made this choice for substantive and practical reasons, as described in Chapter Five.

Our discussion of ML and its relationship with Truth Decay is also inclusive in other ways. We focus on both production and consumption of media and explore what we know about ML in relation to various different contexts and different forms of media—print, television, social media (e.g., Twitter, Facebook), digital journalism (e.g., online sites for such traditional media outlets as the *Wall Street Journal*, CNN, or the *Washington Post*), and digital-only publications (e.g., Huffington Post, Breitbart, or Medium). Although our research and analysis is heavily focused on the U.S. context, we also consider some literature from a more international context. We do, however, limit our inventory of ML resources to those that are U.S.-developed and focused, although we acknowledge seminal work done outside of the United States.

---

[10] We define a competency as "the ability of an individual to mobilize and use internal resources such as knowledge, skills and attitudes, as well as external resources such as databases, colleagues, peers, libraries, tools, and instruments, among others, in order to solve a specific problem efficiently in a real-life situation," as defined by the United Nations Educational, Scientific and Cultural Organization (UNESCO). UNESCO, *Global Media and Information Literacy Assessment Framework: Country Readiness and Competencies*, Paris, 2013).

A Theory of Action for Media Literacy and Truth Decay

One of the key objectives for this report is to determine whether ML education could be useful in counteracting the broader consequences of what we are calling Truth Decay. RAND's initial report on Truth Decay explores the causes and consequences of the phenomenon.[11] At least two of the causes are directly tied to ML. First, the 2018 report describes several changes in the information system that might be contributing to Truth Decay and are also directly related to ML: the rise of the internet and social media, changes in the economics of media (e.g., increased competition from diverse sources and shrinking profit margins), the role played by filters and algorithms, and simply the volume and speed with which information flows. The initial report also describes the role of the education system, specifically the competing demands and institutional characteristics of the education system that challenge its ability to rapidly incorporate changes that would be needed to fully prepare students for the evolving informational environment. The consequences of Truth Decay are the erosion of civil discourse, political paralysis, individual alienation and disengagement, and policy uncertainty at a national level. Finally, the 2018 report identifies several different courses of action that might mitigate the spread and consequences of Truth Decay in the long term, one of which involves the deepening and institutionalization of ML education across the United States.[12] Figure 1.1 illustrates the basic Truth Decay framework.

With this framework as a backdrop, there appear to be several ways in which ML might be able to counter Truth Decay. First, by building capacity to evaluate reliability and credibility of information, ML education could help participants gauge what sources to trust in the midst of increasing disagreement about facts, empirical evidence, and their relative importance. By learning to create and share information in ways reflective of credibility, participants might contribute

---

[11] Kavanagh and Rich, 2018.

[12] We do not provide detail on these different elements of the original Truth Decay framework here, but the report itself contains extensive explanation. See Kavanagh and Rich, 2018.

Figure 1.1
Truth Decay as a System

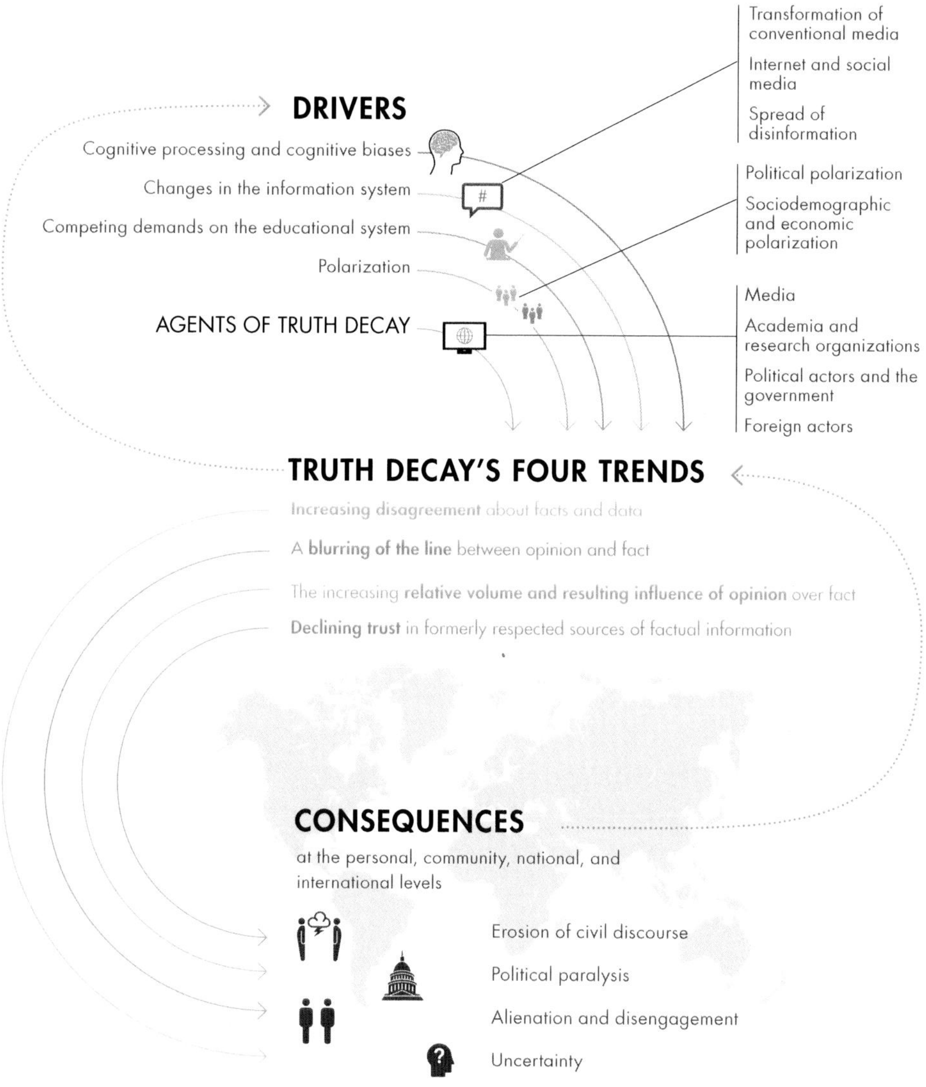

SOURCE: Kavanagh and Rich, 2018.

less to the disinformation and misinformation loop. ML also might contribute to rebuilding trust in institutions, such as those in the fields of journalism and scientific research, by teaching participants about the technical expertise and rigorous behind-the-scenes processes that contribute to publishing respected products in these fields. Such insights might help to distinguish those journalistic or research institutions that abide by accepted standards of practice from those that do not. Relatedly, understanding how the economics of media affect the framing, transmission, and targeting of information can help in understanding potential bias. Building these capacities will never completely eliminate discrepancies in the interpretation of information, but doing so might develop critical thinking and communication skills that can foster agreement around the nature and quality of evidence. Each of these possible benefits of ML education speaks directly to one or more factors contributing to Truth Decay.

Approach, Audience, and Limitations of This Project

Approach

This project involved collecting and analyzing information in three ways, pursued in parallel. The first way was to conduct interviews with 12 experts in ML and related fields who provided information regarding the conceptualization of ML as a field of study, available programs, the evolution and practical challenges of the field, development and delivery of educational programming, and the achievement and evaluation of impact. The second method was to review empirical research documenting results from studies of ML interventions. The third task was to develop an inventory of current ML resources available to the public, focusing this final strand of our work on news and information literacy. We synthesized this information to better understand how ML is conceptualized in the field, the degree to which empirical evidence supports the use of ML interventions, and gaps in our knowledge that might hinder the ability of ML education to serve as a counterweight to Truth Decay. Throughout the report, we relate key insights to implications for the relationship between Truth Decay and ML, and we offer several recommendations for further research. We describe our methods, as appropriate, in each chapter.

Audience

We are writing for several audiences. First, we hope this report will be of value to all those seeking solutions to the extensive societal challenges posed by misinformation, disinformation, and bias. This report is written in a manner that we hope is digestible for this wide audience. Second, we seek to reach educators—formal and informal and across disciplines—who are interested in better understanding how ML education is situated within the broader field, or in expanding the existing role of ML in their practice. Finally, we hope this report speaks to researchers like ourselves, from divergent backgrounds—education, political science, and technology—who have not previously investigated the topic of ML but are motivated to explore solutions and responses to some of the challenges in our current media ecosystem.[13] For these communities, we offer a summary and synthesis of key debates in the ML field, a summary of literature on ML interventions, and a review of relevant measures. For researchers already engaged in studies related to ML, we offer an external perspective on what steps might continue moving work ahead in this field.

Limitations

As noted throughout this introduction, ML as a field has a broad scope, encompassing many ways in which individuals construct and deconstruct information. Given this scope, we are unable to attend to all domains within ML with the degree and level of detail that they each deserve. Our primary focus in this report is on those applications most relevant to the phenomenon of Truth Decay: news and information literacy and, to some extent, digital literacy. Our focus on these fields is not exclusive; we also survey literature from the broader ML field as

---

[13] These parties might find of interest other RAND reports on the topic. See Kavanagh and Rich, 2018; and Jennifer Kavanagh, William Marcellino, Jonathan S. Blake, Shawn Smith, Steven Davenport, and Mahlet G. Tebeka, *News in a Digital Age: Comparing the Presentation of News Information over Time and Across Media Platforms*, Santa Monica, Calif.: RAND Corporation, RR-2960-RC, 2019.

relevant to our research questions and seek to understand how insights from studies of ML related to health, violence, advertising, and other areas might be applicable to our research questions. Still, it would be impossible to do justice to the full body of research or to interview all of the diverse range of experts in the ML field with the resources available for this single report. We recognize that there are related literacies and literatures not surveyed here, and ML resources outside of our scope that were not included in our inventory. These are high-priority topics for future research.

Structure of This Report

The remainder of the report is organized as follows. Chapter Two draws on our interviews with experts in the field and digs deeper into many of the issues raised in this introductory chapter: key debates, stakeholders, assessment of ML outcomes, and other open questions. Chapter Three provides an overview of research related to ML interventions and identifies gaps in the literature. Chapter Four focuses on assessment, describing several approaches used to measure ML competencies in extant research. Chapter Five offers an inventory of publicly available ML resources, such as curricula for teachers and parents; this chapter is more narrowly scoped, focusing only on news and information literacy. In each chapter, we tie key insights and lessons learned through our research to the topic at hand—the degree to which ML holds promise to mitigate the spread of Truth Decay. In the final chapter, we identify areas in which further investment would facilitate progress in the ML field.

CHAPTER TWO

Insights from Interviews with ML Experts

As noted in the introduction, the fields of ML and related literacies have many overlapping definitions and a broad scope that continues to evolve with the changing information ecosystem. In addition to divergent views about how best to define ML, researchers and practitioners in the field have differing views about how best to teach ML and how to assess ML competencies. Given this lack of consensus, it was important for us to gain a better understanding of the field by speaking with the experts who work in it. Our interviews with ML experts explored key debates, best practices, and central open questions in ML education. We conducted interviews with 12 experts and used that information to identify key issues and insights that could anchor our understanding of ML and guide our continuing analysis.

Methodology

Protocol and Focus

Our interviews were guided by our research questions and informed by our review of the literature and survey of ML programs, both of which were ongoing as we developed protocol and conducted interviews. In our protocol, we focused on definitions, asking how the respondent would define ML and what is included within that title. Second, we discussed ML as a field, asking about the key issues, gaps, or challenges that stood out to the respondent. Third, we discussed best practices in ML education as determined by the respondent's expertise and experience. Finally, we asked about assessment and evaluation, focusing on whether the respondent felt existing modes of assessment and evaluation were sufficient, and how the assessment of ML skills could be improved. More broadly, we sought to learn about the ML landscape in order to better situate our work.

Our interview protocol was semistructured, allowing for flexibility depending on interviewee background. We first generated a generic list of questions rooted in the framing of our inquiry. Prior to interviewing each expert, we reviewed their background and research and updated the protocol to better suit that person's expertise. Interviews lasted between 30 and 60 minutes, depending on scheduling constraints.

Interview Sample and Recruitment

We employed three primary sampling techniques to identify experts for the interview portion of our work. First, we focused on people who were frequently cited in our preliminary review of relevant literature; these were typically academics and researchers from across a variety of disciplines. Second, we used the ongoing search of ML resources (presented in Chapter Five) to generate a list of experts and practitioners. We included individuals who were listed as occupying influential positions in developing or implementing ML resources, many of whom had demonstrated long-term engagement in the field. Finally, we asked interviewees for suggestions of other experts whom they thought would be most informative for our study. These three approaches generated an initial list of 21 individuals representing a variety of private and nonprofit corporations invested in ML, as well as academics from a diverse set of disciplines, such as journalism, education, and philosophy.

From this list of 21, we prioritized interviewees whose work was most directly relevant to our interest in ML as it relates to Truth Decay. We offered interviewees confidentiality. We stopped inviting interviewees when we felt we had saturation regarding the major themes we were interested in, on which we found a great deal of agreement across sectors and disciplines. We concluded with 12 expert interviewees engaged in ML. This is by no means an exhaustive list of experts engaged with the issues of media and related literacies, and in future iterations of this work, we intend to expand the number and variety of interviewees. The 12 experts in our sample are leading researchers in the ML field and practitioners or organizational leaders involved in the development and teaching of ML courses.

Analysis

Once interviews were complete, we transcribed them and uploaded the transcripts into Dedoose, a qualitative analysis software.[1] Dedoose allowed us to analyze our transcripts and code for themes in order to identify patterns, similarities, and insights across interviews, using both deductive and inductive codes. We developed a set of codes based on key themes that emerged from our literature review and review of programs but also added new codes based on unanticipated themes that emerged in multiple interviews. When a theme arose across the majority of interviews or appeared to carry particular importance, a team member wrote a one- to two-page memo summarizing the key points offered by the experts. We used these memos to inform the discussion of key themes presented in this chapter.

Surveying the ML Landscape: Definitions, Stakeholders, and Tensions

Our interviews broadly oriented us to the ML field and informed our ongoing literature and resource searches. In this section, we discuss three core themes that emerged from our conversations: the landscape of the ML field, the evolution of ML as a field, and the relationships among ML, critical thinking, and trust.

Defining the ML Field

We noted in Chapter One that there are varied opinions about what specific competencies ML encompasses, how it relates to literacy more broadly and specifically to subdisciplines such as news literacy and information literacy. Our interviews provided insight and context into

---

[1] In the case of three interviews, we used only interview notes. We include quotes in this report only from interviews that were professionally transcribed.

ongoing discussions about how ML is conceptualized, how it connects to other related topics, and how it should be studied.

Most interviewees agreed that ML has a broad remit, covering the study of all forms of media, such as how media messages are constructed, interpreted, and shared. One interviewee described ML as the ability to reflect and act on information. In defining ML broadly, another interviewee suggested that, "It's a bigger picture of how we inhabit a complex media environment, and how do we learn to be meaningful participants in that environment, how we take in information, the choices we make about what information to spread, and choices to make about what information is real. We need all those integrated together." Interviewees emphasized that ML should not be considered a passive activity or an activity based on only information consumption. Instead, every participant should be treated as an active and engaged contributor in the media ecosystem.

Within the broad field of ML, interviewees identified several related subdisciplines, three of which are particularly relevant to our investigation of the relationship between ML and Truth Decay: news literacy, information literacy, and digital literacy. News literacy differs from ML writ large, according to interviewees, in that it is focused on news information and is rooted in journalism and, to an extent, civics. One interviewee told us that news literacy is grounded in the competencies of ML, but that, "In news literacy, you also have critical-thinking skills that encompass the culture of journalism, that encompass civics, that is related to news, the First Amendment, and a free press." Another said that news literacy is a "tributary" of ML, with a narrower focus. In contrast, information literacy, according to interviewees, is more about being able to find and locate information (digital and other types), and emphasizes the skills needed to navigate the information ecosystem, such as the roles played by algorithms and filters. Interviewees also discussed digital literacy, which focuses on the ability to navigate, interpret, analyze, and contribute to information on the internet. Digital literacy is an essential part of ML because people increasingly consume information via online channels. One interviewee emphasized that digital literacy encompasses only one important strand of knowledge and competencies that individuals need, and not the gamut of ML competencies. This expert argued, "ML needs to be larger than the digital. The digital is an important space, it's a place where change is happening, but [. . .] I don't think you can understand the digital as an abstraction from so-called legacy media or mass media; we need to have access to all the tools and all the media, the whole media system."

Ultimately, the subfields remain interwoven. One interviewee described the relationships among these different subfields this way:

> Librarians are a big player for digital and information literacy and a lot of that is about being able to do Google searches well, tell good websites and bad websites, that goes back to the '90s, but it's very strong now, and it cuts into research skills. So just from a practical sense, you learn that in your English language arts curriculum. [. . .] News literacy is different because it's about the news media and it connects to politics and voting, therefore you can put it in the civics curriculum, which is a different part of the school and a different field. [. . .] So, it gets taught in different parts of the school. And there are different constituencies, and it kind of bleeds into different professions.

In addition to noting these variations, interviewees pointed to the overlapping yet competing subfields as unnecessary divisions among researchers and practitioners. Such divisions can, in the extreme, constrain the ability of the field to make substantive progress on key issues. As one individual explained,

> For instance, the scholars in education, they're not reading the communication literature. Those folks who are doing news literacy, they're not reading the education literature, they're just reading within journalism. So, the fragmentation and the disciplinary silos have contributed a lot to the diverse terms and terminology that you have encountered. But the historical progression, and the disciplinary stakeholders, [make it] very hard to read across all these communities.

Another echoed this sentiment, saying, "We have a lot of different factions within the field of media literacy. [. . . A] lot of the news literacy people don't really accommodate the media literacy [people] and vice versa. And what we really need to do is bring together all of these elements, so we need everything, we need it all in order to really face what's happening in this news-media ecosystem."

Interviewees varied in their assessment of the relative importance of different aspects of ML. Some felt that too much emphasis on media criticism was the wrong way to approach ML, for instance, because of the way it can permanently and universally erode institutional trust. Others felt that too much focus on news literacy—and what they perceived to be a related push for "fact-checking"—were potentially problematic, largely because both are imbued with a specific conception of investigative journalism, and because they divert attention away from other key ML topics. Such disagreements around focal points of the interrelated literacies can appear as "turf battles," particularly because the different groups are often competing with one another for funding. One expert told us,

> One of the problems in all of this, which I'd put it in the category of pointless turf battles, is people using different expressions for these literacies, and fighting for the funding which has been quite limited. [. . .] That's reality. And I think that people are starting to realize that instead of fighting over the money, we should be working together.

We discuss these discrepancies to highlight the complexity of the ML field and because the divisions between subfields have implications for research and the degree to which we are able to aggregate findings related to ML. We note, though, that there are benefits to having a variety of disciplines contributing to this field of study, as well, because each offers a unique perspective. In this vein, several experts told us about areas in which they have seen promise of cooperation and convergence, such as past academic and practitioner forums that featured varied streams of ML. More collaboration might move the field forward in meaningful ways, as we will discuss in later chapters.

The Evolution of ML as a Field

The evolution of media itself has contributed to changes in the ML field. When discussing how and why ML has evolved over time, interviewees identified two key changes: (1) shifts related to technological and digital advancements and (2) increased attention to and research in the field.

Technological changes have played a key role in propelling ML to its current state, more directed toward the production and creation of media than it has been in the past. One interviewee commented that, "In the classroom, in the olden days, it [ML] was really focused on deconstruction." Today, construction has become a more central emphasis. In our conversations, an expert explained how access to technology has contributed to the need for these shifts, saying, "Technology has evolved, we basically have the means of production right in our hands with smart phones, and so now in the classroom there's a lot more emphasis on production." Describing what this emphasis looks like, another expert remarked that educators need to "Treat students not just as consumers, but as creators [. . .] whether they are posting, texting, blogging, they're part of the conversation. So how do they play these roles in ways that are responsible, credible, and empower their voices?" Technology has also modernized the delivery of ML education, giving educators new teaching tools and facilitating new strategies. At least one interviewee found this shift to be empowering: "It's much more possible now in a normal classroom to really be able to teach media literacy in kind of a full evolution, because the technology permits it and there's a lot more understanding of what it's really about." The experts we interviewed generally communicated these changes as positive developments.

A second change noted was a recent increase in attention to the field and in the number of researchers and practitioners working in it. ML and related subfields have developed over decades but now appear to be garnering additional attention. This could be in part a result of rising concerns about such issues as misinformation, disinformation, bias, and the challenges they present to our democratic systems. Several interviewees phrased the gap between the requirements of our media ecosystem and the skills of our populace broadly as an emergency, with one saying, "I think people realize that we can't go on this way. We have to do something." The urgency has brought with it some benefits for the field. One interviewee made clear the advantages that have come with increased relevance and attention:

> I would say in general I feel we've gone from being a voice in the wilderness to an answer to a prayer, in that initially I had to spend a lot of time explaining what news literacy was and why it mattered and why people should support it or get involved with it. I don't have to do that anymore. The world around us has changed so dramatically that somebody said to me, "the world has come to us." [. . .] There are many, many more players in the field, both domestically and internationally. And we found a lot more interest and a lot more support for our mission, which has been allowing us to grow quite dramatically now.

But it is possible that this heightened attention has contributed to challenges in the form of yet more competing ideas and sometimes disagreements. Another expert noted, "It's exciting to know there are so many people doing awesome work but also a little overwhelming, because I think people all have different ideas of what works, and also how you measure it is a question." The question of measures is one we return to in Chapter Four. Interviewees generally agreed that the changing media ecosystem has raised the stakes and made ML more essential than ever before. One ML expert described the critical need for ML in a changing world as follows:

> I think it's a crucial skill for life in the 21st century. Public schools were set up to provide the basic skills citizens need to function in an American democracy, so those included the ability to read and write, to do math, to be aware of how the government operated and so forth. [. . .] In the 21st century, so many of our core institutions and practices are conducted through media, television as well as digital media, [. . .] interactive media. That means if we're going to continue to function as public education to prepare citizens for democratic [participation], they need to have core skills in understanding how media works and how to effectively communicate their messages through media, how to sort out fact and

> fiction within media, and how media shapes the institutions and practices of their everyday lives.

Some experts, however, worried that both technological changes and increasing attention to ML as a response to the spread of disinformation online might have some negative implications for ML as a field. Chief among these was the growing trend of equating ML primarily or exclusively with "fact-checking" rather than considering the broader themes and insights that really define and characterize ML. Several interviewees emphasized that although checking the veracity of information is critical, it should not be privileged over other essential ML skills and tasks, such as deconstructing media holistically, studying media creation, and looking for varied sources of media bias. From the perspective of our research questions, this is an important point. Even as we consider the ways in which ML education might work to counter the trends of Truth Decay, we must not lose sight of the broader field of ML and the diverse set of competencies it encompasses.

In emphasizing what has changed, it is also worth mentioning what has remained the same. Interviewees reported that ML is fundamentally about thinking critically, and not about any specific context or topic. Even as the media environment continues to evolve, the core competencies of ML are likely to remain the same.

Balancing Critical Thinking and Trust

Several of our expert interviewees told us that ML should be considered a holistic worldview, a way to think, and a way to process and interpret information. ML encompasses a set of critical thinking competencies that can be applicable across subjects and contexts. As one interviewee explained, "Media literacy should be central to education, not on the periphery. [. . .] It's not a new subject to teach, it's a new way to teach all subjects." Another provided a more detailed vision of ML, describing how it could be integrated throughout existing courses:

> I think what you want is a paradigm shift where media literacy skills are incorporated across the entire disciplines, all of the disciplines in the school day, integrating it into how we teach the core subjects, so the social science teacher takes ownership of some

> skills, the science teacher takes ownership of other skills and throughout the school day it simply becomes part of how people think about the world around them in an integrated way rather than one more thing the schools have to do in addition to all the other subjects they already teach.

Another expert told us, "ML doesn't teach us what to think, just how to think." However, the experts we interviewed differed in the specific competencies that they defined as making up this core set of critical thinking skills. For one of them, integrating critical thinking meant focusing on principles of journalism—skepticism, using informed judgment, asking questions, and assessing information-collecting processes. To another, integrating critical thinking meant giving participants opportunities to "explore and discuss real-world problems" rather than offering lectures on ML content. One expert took a holistic view, describing ML as "an empowered notion of engaging with media so that you can make conscious choices between what's right and wrong, what's truth and falsehood, what's information and opinion, and also actively contribute to the flow of information, either through things you create and share yourself, or through the choices you make about what to spread through your social media."

Some interviewees reported a tension in balancing analytical questioning and skepticism with an interest in establishing and maintaining trust in credible institutions. Experts agreed this can be a tricky line to navigate. The danger is that the analytic questioning that is core to ML could be taught or interpreted in a way that crosses the boundary into cynicism, damaging trust even in reliable sources of information. If ML participants learn not to trust any media or information at all, rather than learning to discern reliable and fact-based information from its unreliable or more-biased counterparts, then the goal of creating more-attentive and better-informed consumers and producers of media will not be met. One interviewee carefully described this tension:

> Knowledge depends on trust, and dramatic levels of distrust destroy knowledge, but you can also be too trusting. You can be naïve, and you can be trusting of the wrong things. So, I think

> you have to say that the outcome we want is trusting the right things at the right time for the right reason. But in a way, that just displaces the hard question, because I think a good follow-up question is: What's the right thing, what should you trust?

ML educators must make the distinction between healthy skepticism and overall cynicism very clear. Another explained:

> We teach that not all information is created equal and that some of it is more credible and trustworthy than others. We don't tell them what that [the credible information] is or where to find it, we want them to locate it. But I think there are some programs that basically teach that everything is driven by bias and that it's just a matter of figuring out what that bias is.

Thus, the relationship between ML and trust is a critical but delicate one. To reach the right balance, one interviewee suggested that ML must include a focus on the processes that contribute to credible media or informational products, such as news reporting or scientific research. Not all news stories are based on rigorous investigative and reporting practices, for instance. Personal opinions are not of the same value as scientific claims built on thorough research processes. If someone better understands the practices, processes, and professional standards undergirding such claims, they will be better able to distinguish credible information. As this interviewee told us, "We are making the point that this is what they should be looking for, for these standards, and giving them the tools to make those judgments, to find what is credible, not to feel that there's nothing credible." This balance is especially important in consideration of Truth Decay, which comprises not only the spread of biased and misleading information but also declining trust in institutions central to informing the populace, such as credible media organizations and research institutions that adhere to established professional standards. If ML education fosters the competencies necessary to challenge and question information but also undermines trust in institutions, then it might address one aspect of Truth Decay while exacerbating another. This is a key tension to keep in mind for the remainder of this report.

Characteristics of High-Quality ML Education

Another goal of our interviews was to learn what experts believe are characteristic best practices in ML education. We asked interviewees for examples of programs or resources that they believed were high-quality. Although we received few specific answers about resources, interviewees did describe some characteristics of high-quality ML education. In this section, we summarize insights that emerged from these discussions.

Modes of Instruction: Stand-Alone or Integrated?

Interviewees noted that there are a variety of different ways that ML can be taught inside and outside classrooms. We characterize two basic approaches to ML education as stand-alone and integrated. With a *stand-alone approach*, ML is taught in its own course and is focused on exclusively. With an *integrated approach*, ML competencies, programming, and activities are blended with other content areas. This is a simplified dichotomy; in reality, educators might choose strategies located somewhere on the spectrum between these two poles.

Interviewees emphasized that there might not be a "correct" approach but that either one (having a stand-alone course or integrating ML into existing courses) could be effective. They highlighted the advantages and disadvantages of each approach. Speaking about the value of integrating ML into existing coursework, interviewees identified three possible advantages. First, it offers more exposure to ML instruction, presenting it as a worldview and not a separate set of skills, as alluded to previously. Second, an integrated approach provides a model for how students could apply ML skills in different contexts. In discussing this benefit, one expert told us this:

> If [media literacy education] is a special treat for students at the end of the week or it's treated as an elective [. . . then] media literacy education is not going to have the impact it needs to have. I think what you want is a paradigm shift where media literacy skills are incorporated across all of the disciplines in the school day—integrating it into how we teach the core subjects, so throughout the school day it simply becomes part of how people think about the world around them in an integrated way.

An integrated approach also minimizes the need for additional courses and materials in already overburdened schools. One interviewee suggested that an integrated approach to teaching ML might be more practical for schools because it would not require scheduling a stand-alone course within the academic day or be seen as "detracting" from time otherwise devoted to assessed subjects such as Mathematics and English language arts.

Ongoing developments in the field of education, particularly trends in content standards, also could support the integration of ML competencies into core curricular courses in the school setting. A majority of states in the United States have adopted the Common Core State Standards, which stress critical thinking and arguably demonstrate better alignment with principles of ML than preceding cohorts of academic standards.[2] Increasing attention has been paid in recent years to what are often referred to as 21st Century Competencies, which consist of critical thinking, communication, and "learning how to learn," among other proficiencies.[3] Another example of this trend is the International Society for Technology in Education standards, which aim to prepare students to operate in a digital landscape and which are directly relevant to ML.[4] The use of these types of standards to integrate ML and define outcomes is an important step forward that we return to in Chapter Four.

Although ML is often considered most applicable to the areas of language arts and social studies, the skills that it focuses on—such as evaluating sources, understanding biases, and synthesizing information from multiple sources—are relevant to other content areas. For instance, ML competencies can relate to science. This is true in light of Next Generation Science Standards, which include critical thinking

---

[2] National Governors Association Center for Best Practices, Council of Chief State School Officers, *Common Core State Standards*, Washington, D.C., 2010.

[3] Brian M. Stecher and Laura S. Hamilton, *Measuring Hard-to-Measure Student Competencies: A Research and Development Plan*, Santa Monica, Calif.: RAND Corporation, RR-863-WFHF, 2014.

[4] International Society for Technology Education, "ISTE Standards for Students," webpage, undated.

and communication skills.[5] These standards require students to offer supporting evidence for claims, a skill that is also often linked with ML. In a more direct example, ML standards have been developed for arts education, allowing teachers to integrate ML principles and activities in art curricula as well. Each of these sets of competencies and standards provides an opportunity to integrate ML into the design or delivery of a variety of subject areas.

However, the integrated approach is not without its drawbacks. One interviewee commented that "when everyone owns ML, no one owns ML," suggesting that when ML is integrated throughout subjects, especially if teaching them falls to more than one educator, it could unintentionally slip through the cracks. In this case, having a stand-alone course, or allocating responsibility for ML to one specific academic subject (such as language arts), might be preferable because it assigns responsibility and accountability. Furthermore, there might be contexts in which stand-alone curricula are the best option based on context—adults seeking new skills or professional development, for example, might seek out stand-alone courses and workshops.

There are publicly available resources that support both stand-alone courses and a more integrated approach. In addition to teacher training, study guides, and handbooks, there are dozens of developed curricula, courses, and lesson plans to assist teachers who want to build a focused course or who want a set of activities or modules that they can weave into their existing practice. Products range from full-semester or yearlong courses to lesson plans and activities that can be used to supplement existing coursework.[6] We asked interviewees to assess the state of existing courses and educational resources. Their reviews were mixed. Although they pointed to some resources that provide excellent support, they noted that many have limitations. For example, one interviewee said that all preexisting curricula and courses come with their own priorities, which means that some topics are covered at the expense of others. One

---

5 Next Generation Science Standards, "Frequently Asked Questions," webpage, undated; Achieve, Inc., *Next Generation Science Standards: For States, by States: Lead States*, Washington, D.C.: National Academies Press, 2013.

6 We introduce real-world examples of these programs and modules in Chapter Five.

interviewee noted that in some cases, this leads to narrower resources that do not capture the full context or set of competencies embodied by ML. Some curricula focus too little on media production, for example, or get mired in the topic of "fake news" but fail to look at the full media ecosystem. The programs that interviewees spoke of most highly shared several characteristics. They were interactive, involved student discussion and engagement, worked within contexts familiar to the students regardless of age, explicitly targeted creativity, and—most of all—were responsive to student needs. We discuss more best practices in ML education through the remainder of this section.

Interviewees noted that not all educators rely on prepackaged ML courses and curricula. Those who are new to ML might choose to download and apply existing lesson plans or to use a predeveloped curriculum in their classes. Those who are more familiar with the concepts of ML might adapt existing programming to fit their academic content or to meet the unique needs of their students. Teachers also might develop their own curriculum and activities and assess the value of those activities independently, modifying them as needed. It is difficult to directly compare these approaches, but as we will discuss in more detail, teachers' skills related to ML competencies do seem to matter, in the estimation of the experts we interviewed. One interviewee emphasized the importance of teacher training.

Notably, although we focus heavily here on ML education provided through schools, there are curricula, workshops, and online activities aimed at adults, including those aimed at specialized populations, such as journalists. We provide a review of a subset of these programs, specifically those covering news and information literacy, in Chapter Five.

The Question of Context

Experts emphasized that the most-effective ML strategies are those that reach participants in a format and context with which they are familiar and comfortable. For example, several interviewees mentioned that one of the shortcomings of existing approaches to ML is the failure to make use of already existing media and advertising to provide ML education, especially to adults. One noted, "I believe the big missed opportunity out there is teaching media literacy through the media, through advertising, just like teaching any other ideas." Others pointed to specific shows on television or radio broadcasts that could be used as teaching tools for adults. Another pointed to the potential role of other institutions: "I think we need to think about it more aggressively through museums, libraries, public institutions, which will reach at least some adults who want to go to continue to learn and grow, right? A lifetime learning model depends on those public institutions."

The same principles apply to students in K–12 schools and universities. Interviewees emphasized the importance of "meet[ing] students where they are at." Several interviewees stressed that the context in which ML is taught can be modified without compromising the core competencies. If students are frequently engaging in video games or heavily consumed with viewing YouTube videos, then educators might be able to make use of those media in teaching ML competencies. For example, one expert advised that if participants spend time engaging with viral videos in their daily lives, using such videos as a tool for communicating the tenets of ML could improve understanding. To give another example, if participants in ML education typically access news and information through a social media platform, such as Facebook, connecting a lesson to that platform in some way could provide a concrete example of how ML skills could be applied in their daily lives. We recognize there are inherent risks in major corporations dictating what constitutes ML—and that is not what we are advocating—but there may be space to leverage their platforms for educational purposes.

One challenge of ML content is making it relevant to a variety of audiences—what is applicable for high school students in California might not be well-suited for retirees in Wisconsin—yet ML would be most effective societally if it reached everyone. As one interviewee said, ML should be widespread in order to build "herd immunity" to such media-related problems as misinformation, disinformation, and bias. Integrating examples and media that are relevant to participants' interests might help accomplish such immunity. This means that each ML course should be unique, shaped not only by the educator providing it but also, and even more importantly, by the participants.

However, this goal is complicated in our current political environment, a fact that interviewees readily pointed out and agreed with. One interviewee noted that ML education, to be successful, must be rigorously nonideological—especially when it comes to news and information literacy. We were told that nonpartisanship was of primary importance, but interviewees had different ways of ensuring this in their own work and teaching. One interviewee commented that he and his colleagues take on charged political issues in the coursework they develop, but they do so in a nonpartisan way and seek feedback from across the political spectrum to ensure a balance. Another noted that she incorporated sources from many different political ideologies in her practice. Others argued that as long as ML education focused on teaching students which questions to ask and how to look for answers, rather than teaching them what those answers are, ML competencies should be noncontroversial. Still another suggested that politicization could be avoided by thinking carefully about the messengers used. For example, having students teach each other through conversation rather than relying on adult educators is one approach. Relying on other, already trusted messengers (such as religious or community leaders) might be another.

Agents Delivering ML Education

Interviewees talked about the facilitators or agents providing ML education broadly, naming teachers, librarians, community and religious leaders, parents, and even journalists. This diverse group of educators is necessary, given the ubiquitous role of media in all stages of individuals' lives. In this section, we discuss the two kinds of agents most often referenced in our interviews—parents and teachers—and whether the experts we interviewed felt the government has a role to play in this work.

When asked where we start in building population-wide immunity to disinformation and bias, one interviewee noted,

> We have to start in kindergarten, we have to start even before that, we have to start with parents in groups, because it has to become internalized, what we're talking about, just as we learn

> to read and write, just as we learn print literacy, we have to learn media literacy, it's more important now than ever.

Another confirmed this view, focusing again on the role that parents can play and the conception of ML as lifelong learning:

> We take the position that media literacy education starts with birth. Children are immersed with different forms of media from the time they're born. And so, they need to start understanding it from an early age, parents need to be equipped with that knowledge as well. In that sense we don't see it as being age related, it really needs to start very early, because [. . .] it's about making sense of the world, and that's what children are going to do.

Parents, then, play a key role in ML education because they can lead this education even in children's early years. Although we did not find many ML programs designed for parents to use specifically with their children (see Chapter Five), the research indicates that improvements in parents' own ML competencies could also improve the competencies of their children.[7]

Interviewees also emphasized the crucial importance of having teachers who are trained in ML and able to integrate its competencies into coursework. Speaking from their own experiences, several interviewees described ways that both teachers and students benefit when teachers are trained well in providing ML education. In describing the type of teacher training likely to be most effective, one expert noted that, rather than providing prepackaged ML curricula as a way to support teachers, an effective approach might be to teach them ML competencies and general strategies, and how they can be applied in varied subject areas. An individual trained in this method, the expert argued, would be able to teach ML in a variety of contexts and courses.

Some teachers lack the resources or institutional support required to fully leverage ML, to take courses aimed at improving their ML

---

[7] Jonathan S. Comer, Jami M. Furr, Rinad S. Beidas, Courtney L. Weiner, and Philip C. Kendall, "Children and Terrorism-Related News: Training Parents in Coping and Media Literacy," *Journal of Consulting and Clinical Psychology*, Vol. 76, No. 4, August 2008.

instruction, or to embrace new teaching methods aimed at promoting ML competencies. One interviewee stated,

> I think the biggest [. . .] problem [is one] of scale and systemic change versus individual change. So, an individual teacher who finds the faith, who becomes convinced in media literacy, it's part of what they want to do, and has access to a variety of resources, if they can find their way to them, but they may face resistance in their own school, taking school time away from preparing for standardized tests or meeting the national standards, to bring media literacy into the classroom. They're not going to get the support of the principals in many cases [. . .] they're not going to get the professional development training they need, they're often going to be looked at with suspicion by their fellow teachers. That sense of sticking your head out too far is a real risk for those educators.

Another interviewee said that at some institutions, "Media literacy has always been seen as something optional. It's not been seen as something that is essential to the curriculum, whatever grade you're talking about. [Those who do teach it] teach the core concepts, but they don't apply it throughout the semester. [. . .] You have to integrate that. [. . .] They [ML competencies] have to become a life skill."

In addition to teachers and parents, several interviewees responded to the question of what role the government and policymakers should play in ML education, with decidedly mixed answers. While recognizing the potential upside of raising the profile and scale of ML education efforts, one expert also pointed to past examples where government involvement in mandated educational standards was particularly controversial.[8] Other interviewees expressed concerns about having the government too involved in deciding how and what should be taught under the guise of ML. One apt expression of these mixed sentiments regarding government involvement came from an interviewee who noted,

---

[8] Government involvement in reading education during the 1990s was used as an example. For a review of this issue, see David Davenport and Jeffrey Jones, "The Politics of Literacy," *Policy Review*, Vol. 130, No. 2, 2005.

> One thing that's starting to happen that could be good, or could not be good, is regulations or mandates from government to teach media literacy. I firmly believe media literacy as a defined set of competencies should be incorporated into state curriculum, but I have an issue with mandating that in the sort of judicial or legislative way, because then I feel like you've got government and politicians potentially being the arbiters of our media literacy.

As some states and municipalities in the United States have recently adopted ML-related mandates, it will be critical to continue to monitor the ways that such mandates are implemented and learn from their experiences. The key insight that emerges from this discussion of agents is that ML education should not be conceived of as occurring only in the classroom. Parents play a key role, as do other agents that were mentioned less frequently in our interviews, such as museums, libraries, religious institutions, and even tech platforms and journalists. If ML is to be a fundamental life skill, then ML education must be woven through out daily activities and interactions.

What Is Required to "Scale" ML Education?

We heard from interviewees that one of the biggest challenges in the field of ML is the need for scale—that is, the ability to reach a much wider audience. Interviewees were not overly optimistic about the prospects for achieving scale in the near term, citing such obstacles as a lack of institutional support and resources, a dearth of ML training for teachers, and an educational system that is already stretched. One interviewee alluded to a general resistance to moving away from rote modes of education, noting, "I'm unfortunately extremely skeptical that we will ever achieve scale [. . .] not because it's a bad idea, but it's improbable that it would become a universal thing in this country for the simple reason that a lot of people in this country think critical thinking is kind of a radical concept." Despite this, several of the experts we interviewed had ideas for ways of working toward this goal.

One interviewee argued that achieving scale would require reconceptualizing ML education as something that happens not primarily in schools, but in spaces of everyday life—libraries, churches, museums, homes, community gatherings, and through both conventional and new media. One expert explained, "Scale starts with education, and education is not something that starts in grade one and ends in grade 12 or after college, it goes on throughout life. [. . .] If we can get scale there, that's a good start." Other interviewees focused on ways that scale within the educational system might be achieved. For example, one suggested that the key was to build flexible educational resources, modules that could be easily integrated rather than displacing existing coursework or creating new requirements, both of which might raise resistance and create new obstacles. This practitioner noted about their work, "We didn't create an elective, we didn't create a whole course, we created basically drop-in units that can be modified and adapted to what teachers are doing [. . .] and that's been a key, because teachers are very stretched and they've got a lot of demands on their plate." We were told that teachers' training and support were important to achieving scale: "That's another key, is to work with educators, not just hand them something, but show them how to use it and maximize the benefit. I think that's been really important in growing the numbers."

Other experts emphasized the role of outside actors in achieving scale. Notably, these actors included tech platforms, such as Facebook and Google. More than one interviewee remarked that these platforms could be important allies because of the scale they have already achieved. Interviewees noted that although such platforms as Twitter and Facebook can contribute to the spread of misinformation and disinformation, their role in the solution is likely "essential." Asked how social media and tech platforms might be able to contribute, several interviewees pointed to transparency, such as making application programming interfaces more transparent. Another suggested that such companies as Facebook, Twitter, and Google could provide users with a variety of additional tools and plugins to assess source credibility. Yet another interviewee suggested a public awareness campaign that would allow the platforms to take advantage of their scale to raise awareness about ML and best practices. The role of media companies and tech platforms in ML education would need to focus on competencies and processes, not on informational content, however, given concerns around these institutions actively deciding what is credible and what is not for the general public.

Conventional media, such as newspapers, magazines, and television, also could play a role in achieving scale. Media outlets could provide more transparency and detail to users regarding their processes, said one interviewee, which would assist users in gauging the credibility of information. Being straightforward about how news and research is funded, the number of sources used, and the review process could build credibility. In the case of journalistic organizations, one interviewee suggested, "Let's give [the audience] a full story and explain to them [. . .] how we arrived at this information, and kind of give them the benefit of the doubt that if they want to know more about why Bob is the source in this story, we can provide that information." Other experts we spoke with pointed to the ways in which conventional media might already be helping ML to become more widespread—for example, through such popular shows as "Adam Ruins Everything," which deconstructs information and asks how we know the things we know, or through such outlets as PBS, which provides some ML education to users through its programming.

Assessing ML Competencies

The final matter we discussed with interviewees was how ML competencies can be assessed and how outcomes of ML interventions should be measured. Interviewees agreed that the areas of assessment and evaluation of ML remain underdeveloped, but also pointed to areas in which progress is being made. As one expert noted, "There hasn't been enough research into the [questions], does this do anything for people, do they come out with better understanding of how the world works and what's going on in their communities, and a better understanding of how media operate? [. . .] That's the thing we have to do, is find out." Another expert described roadblocks to assessing ML competencies in the following way:

> Assessment is challenging, because what we've seen so far is we're finding media literacy programs when they work are fostering skills that we don't yet have good measures for. So, when we try to

> do standardized testing, we probably underestimate the amount of impact media literacy education can have, because we don't know how to count, measure, quantify, scale up [those] kinds of behavior. We don't have good tests for it.

In other words, media literacy programs might work in ways and have impacts that are not yet fully known. This interviewee expected that this might lead to an undervaluing of ML education and the effect it could have on participants. A few interviewees agreed with this summary assessment but also noted ways that they had been working to fill this gap, collecting data on student skills and knowledge before and after ML courses and activities. They reported that their evaluations indicated improvement in ML competencies following those courses, but they did not specify what metrics they used, and we did not have in-depth discussions about their methodology or results.[9]

Assessing ML competencies and evaluating ML curricula are both more challenging tasks than they might seem on the surface. Assessment in the ML field, interviewees explained, requires a nuanced approach precisely because ML is often conceived of as a holistic set of skills that are most relevant in their application rather than when taken independent of context. To truly assess ML competencies and to know whether an ML course "worked," researchers must be able to observe the degree to which participants are able to apply and use ML skills in the context of everyday life. One interviewee described,

> It's not what they've learned, it's how they apply it. Because what you're really talking about is a life skill. It's a tool that you're going to use throughout the life cycle. [. . .] So a way you can measure [is] with standardized tests and all of that, but another way to measure it is through reflection and through a more qualitative than quantitative analysis, which on a large scale would be really challenging.

Another expert that we interviewed commented that the type of assessment framework required to evaluate these skills "in application"

---

9 We discuss existing research on ML intervention outcomes in more detail in Chapter Three.

would be more sophisticated than what currently exists. As one noted of assessment, "We don't [do more assessment] because it would take a new generation of assessment, so in particular there's a real gap for news and the assessment of processing of news and current events. And it really comes down to some practicalities that could be overcome, but there's no investment in overcoming it."

Thus, the picture that we take away from our interviews with regard to the issue of measuring ML competencies is mixed. Assessment is on the minds of experts in the field. Several are currently active in this area, working to collect data and assess student progress. Experts recognize that a gap exists, both in the identification of metrics and the execution of assessments and evaluations, but they are also cognizant that ML competencies require more than a traditional standardized test. In Chapter Four, we discuss existing assessment strategies we found in the ML literature and describe the pros and cons of each as they apply to ML broadly as well as the specific competencies that we are most interested in.

Summary

In this chapter, we have described key themes and insights that surfaced from interviews with ML experts. Several important takeaways emerge. First, ML is best defined as the ability to identify, assess, analyze, interpret, create, reflect, and act on media of all types. Within the broader umbrella of ML, news literacy, information literacy, and digital literacy—in addition to other, related literacies—have more-focused apertures, although they involve overlapping competencies. Some interviewees emphasized that ML is best conceived of as a holistic worldview, a way of thinking that permeates all interactions with information, rather than sets of discrete skills. Second, the ML field is evolving, becoming increasingly focused on fact-checking and digital media. This aspect of ML has garnered additional attention in recent years, but interviewees stressed that it is important not to lose focus on the broader competencies of ML. Our interviews also covered best practices in ML education, first exploring the debate between stand-alone and integrated ML curricula. Integrating ML into other courses, in the case of K–12 and postsecondary education, might offer some unique benefits; ultimately, however, we do not have evidence to support one approach over another. Other best practices were attending to context, personalizing programs to match the participant population, and ensuring parents and teachers are supported in ML education. We also discussed the issue of scale—that is, how ML education can achieve a scale and scope that builds broad immunity to misinformation, disinformation, and bias across the population. Interviewees pointed to the role that media and tech companies could play, if responsibly implemented. Finally, we considered assessment. Interviewees noted the importance of program evaluation and assessing student outcomes, but also highlighted challenges in doing so, such as the need for new and more sophisticated metrics that can assess complex ML competencies in context. We further discuss the issue of measuring ML competencies in Chapter Four and return to many of the issues raised here again as we move through our exploration and analysis.

CHAPTER THREE

Reviewing Studies of ML Interventions

In Chapter Two, we offered a broad picture of the field based on the perspectives of interviewed researchers, practitioners, and experts engaged in ML and related literacies. In this chapter, we consider empirical literature in order to explore two of our research questions. First, we sought to better understand ways that ML is conceptualized across the field, this time referring to empirical and conceptual literature. How does the research frame ML and related literacies? One way to understand this is through the kinds of outcomes that researchers address in their studies, as we will briefly describe in the first half of this chapter. Second, we explored the extent to which current evidence suggests that ML education could be an appropriate counterbalance to problems of Truth Decay. Does ML work to build participant capacity in relevant competencies and, if so, under what conditions? In answering this question, we identified gaps and opportunities for further research in this field.

We reviewed ML studies that span numerous disciplines, varied methodological approaches, and different contexts, as we will describe. This is beneficial in some ways because the diversity of research related to ML provides a multidimensional view of the subject, adding nuance to our knowledge of the field. Yet, with so many different ways of defining and measuring ML, it is difficult to make meaning of findings across studies. Because of the challenge in systematically aggregating data of this variety, we caution that this overview of literature should be read with its limitations in mind.

Approach

Our process for identifying literature was iterative. We conducted searches in multiple waves; after each round of searching and a review of the corresponding literature, terms were refined and new searches were added. Our original literature search was conducted in multiple electronic databases, including the Education Resource Information Center and Web of Science.[1] We used a diverse set of search terms and combined these terms in different permutations to explore the relevant literature as comprehensively as possible.[2] We also searched for research by specific authors and on specific topics as informed by our reading. Additionally, we relied on reference lists from included work, Google Scholar, and recommendations from colleagues and interviewees. We directly reviewed such ML-related websites as The Florida College System Civics Literacy Initiative, the Center for News Literacy (Stony Brook University), the Media Education Lab (University of Rhode Island), and the News Co/Lab (Arizona State University). We stopped adding new sources at the point when our searches were returning primarily articles we had already included or had intentionally decided to exclude, and when we felt that we could adequately summarize key findings related to the goals of this chapter as previously described.

We primarily included studies that were conducted in the United States. We focused on articles from 2000 or later because we are most interested in ML in the context of the more-complex media and information environment that has developed over the past two decades. However, we also reviewed studies that appeared seminal or filled a unique space in the field, regardless of study location or date.

Research in ML has developed in reference to a broad array of topics—public health, civics education, journalism, and numerous others. We included research addressing all of these topics. We did so in part because the set of studies exclusively addressing outcomes of

---

1 Education Resource Information Center, homepage, undated; Clarivate Analytics, "Web of Science," webpage, undated.

2 Some of these search terms were media literacy, information literacy, news literacy, digital literacy, civics literacy, fake news, critical thinking, education, course, program, effectiveness, outcomes, evaluation, measurement, measures, rubric, and framework.

ML interventions as relevant to Truth Decay–related competencies was too limited for a review. By including examples from this wider field rather than focusing narrowly on any one area, we captured a broad set of insights. We considered studies with quantitative, qualitative, and mixed methods research designs.[3] We considered literature dealing with ML in a variety of contexts, when the research questions or findings contributed to our understanding of associations between ML interventions and Truth Decay–related competencies. Throughout the review, we highlight some of these insights that appeared relevant to our research focus, and we describe these connections in more detail in the final section of this chapter.[4]

Conceptualizations of ML and Related Literacies

To define ML, most of the studies we consulted use the classic, accepted definition that we refer to throughout this report: the ability to access, analyze, evaluate, and communicate messages.[5] However, the way that individual studies frame ML is necessarily more nuanced. Looking across the types of outcomes these studies sought, we identified three primary ways that existing research conceptualizes ML skills and competencies. First, some research conceptualizes ML in relation to the influence of economic drivers on the construction of media messages. A second subset of literature focuses on the role of media in civic life and democracy, and the importance of ML in that context. A final set of studies focuses on ML as a route to better understanding information quality. Clearly, these categories are not mutually exclusive. We

---

[3] This means that a significant portion of the studies included in our review provide only correlational or descriptive evidence. For various reasons described in Chapter Four, a notable proportion of ML research has employed methods other than causal design to evaluate effectiveness.

[4] Despite our broad approach to this review, and given the breadth and variation of literature related to ML education, we will inevitably miss research that others might find relevant. We look forward to broadening the scope of reviewed literature in future projects as we continue to learn and the field continues in its evolution.

[5] Aufderheide, 1993, pp. 9–10.

use these three primary variants of ML as a way to frame our discussion of the ML field, but we emphasize that this is a heuristic—some studies might not fit cleanly within this typology.

The Economic Motivations of Media Construction

A first subset of research frames ML and its competencies in light of the economic motivations that drive media construction. ML scholars applying this approach focus on economic drivers as a central influence shaping the content and medium of the messages that ultimately reach our information ecosystem.

The economic motivations behind media messages are one focus in studies concerning public health.[6] These studies tend to focus on participants' understanding of how entertainment media or advertisers use false or misleading messages to make them feel particular ways or make certain purchases.[7] For instance, in a study exploring the capacity for an ML intervention to change participant perspectives on violence in the media, one of the outcomes measured is participant knowledge about "whether media is based on a desire for influence, profit, and power."[8] A study on the results of an ML program on children's evaluation of unhealthy media messages contains a focal concept that "students understand that all media tell stories and are meant to

---

[6] For more information concerning the link between research in health and ML, see Joan Wharf Higgins and Deborah Begoray, "Exploring the Borderlands Between Media and Health: Conceptualizing Critical Media Health Literacy," *Journal of Media Literacy Education*, Vol. 4, No. 2, 2012.

[7] Erica Weintraub Austin, Bruce E. Pinkleton, Stacey J. T. Hust, and Marilyn Cohen, "Evaluation of an American Legacy Foundation/Washington State Department of Health Media Literacy Pilot Study," *Health Communication*, Vol. 18, No. 1, 2005; Erica Weintraub Austin, Yi-Chun Chen, Bruce E. Pinkleton, and Jessie Quintero Johnson, "Benefits and Costs of Channel One in a Middle School Setting and the Role of Media-Literacy Training," *Pediatrics*, Vol. 117, No. 3, March 2006; David S. Bickham and Ronald G. Slaby, "Effects of a Media Literacy Program in the US on Children's Critical Evaluation of Unhealthy Media Messages About Violence, Smoking, and Food," *Journal of Children and Media*, Vol. 6, No. 2, 2012.

[8] Kathryn R. Fingar and Tessa Jolls, "Evaluation of a School-Based Violence Prevention Media Literacy Curriculum," *Injury Prevention*, Vol. 20, No. 3, 2013.

make them feel an emotion, do something, think something, or buy something."[9]

Other studies with an emphasis on economic drivers specifically explore news literacy and ML, addressing the connection between topic choice, how a story is communicated, and economic motivations—including the need to attract and keep viewers or readers. For instance, a study of ML intervention outcomes addresses participants' ability to "recognize the complex blurring of information, entertainment, and economics that are present in contemporary nonfiction media."[10] Another study focuses on how increased knowledge about media ownership influences undergraduate students' perceptions of media credibility.[11] In a study focused on awareness of media structures and economics and critically viewing advertisements, researchers measured outcomes of a course that focused on, among other things, "the basic financial structure of media organizations, including who owns and controls the media, how media profits are made, who pays for content, and how economic considerations affect content."[12] The focal idea in each of these studies is that media messages are driven by economic motivations and that being able to identify and evaluate those motivations is an important aspect of ML education.

The Role of Media in Civic Life and Democracy

Another group of articles frames ML competencies and outcomes in light of civic life and democracy. ML experts subscribing to this conceptualization often focus on critical consumption of media and current events as essential duties of the populace. In these articles, ML

---

[9] Bickham and Slaby, 2012, p. 261.

[10] Renee Hobbs and Richard Frost, "Measuring the Acquisition of Media-Literacy Skills," *Reading Research Quarterly*, Vol. 38, No. 3, 2003, p. 351.

[11] Seth Ashley, Mark Poepsel, and Erin Willis, "Media Literacy and News Credibility: Does Knowledge of Media Ownership Increase Skepticism in News Consumers?" *Journal of Media Literacy Education*, Vol. 2, No. 1, 2010.

[12] Robert L. Duran, Bill Yousman, Kaitlin M. Walsh, and Melanie A. Longshore, "Holistic Media Education: An Assessment of the Effectiveness of a College Course in Media Literacy," *Communication Quarterly*, Vol. 56, No. 1, 2008, pp. 57–58.

is framed as a way to provide participants with the skills necessary to fulfill this responsibility. Some also focus on ways that media could be used as a tool for democratic involvement. Articles that conceptualize ML competencies and outcomes in this way focus on a variety of topics, such as news literacy, digital literacy, and critical media literacy.

We found that news-related studies often frame their research in reference to civic life. One study on a news literacy intervention addresses participants' "perceptions that citizens have a job to be critical consumers of news, and [understanding of] the value that media literacy has for democracy."[13] A pair of news-related ML studies of interest explore predictors of students' "intent toward civic engagement," which refers to students' attitudes toward civic activities, such as volunteering and voting, and publicly expressing political opinions.[14] Another news literacy study examines the extent to which an ML program fosters "greater knowledge of current events, and higher motivation to consume news."[15]

Some digital literacy studies also focus on civic life and democracy. This might be increasingly important in light of the ways that digital media today connect individuals with news and with one another, providing new platforms for civic engagement.[16] One study connects college students' reported exposure to digital literacy with indicators

---

[13] Melissa Tully and Emily K. Vraga, "Effectiveness of a News Media Literacy Advertisement in Partisan Versus Nonpartisan Online Media Contexts," *Journal of Broadcasting and Electronic Media*, Vol. 61, No. 1, 2017, p. 158.

[14] Renee Hobbs, Katie Donnelly, Jonathan Friesem, and Mary Moen, "Learning to Engage: How Positive Attitudes About the News, Media Literacy, and Video Production Contribute to Adolescent Civic Engagement," *Educational Media International*, Vol. 50, No. 4, 2013; Hans Martens and Renee Hobbs, "How Media Literacy Supports Civic Engagement in a Digital Age," *Atlantic Journal of Communication*, Vol. 23, No. 2, 2015.

[15] Adam Maksl, Stephanie Craft, Seth Ashley, and Dean Miller, "The Usefulness of a News Media Literacy Measure in Evaluating a News Literacy Curriculum," *Journalism and Mass Communication Educator*, Vol. 72, No. 2, 2017, p. 228.

[16] Paul Mihailidis and Benjamin Thevenin, "Media Literacy as a Core Competency for Engaged Citizenship in Participatory Democracy," *American Behavioral Scientist*, Vol. 57, No. 11, 2013.

of their online civic and political engagement.[17] Finally, critical media literacy studies often frame ML in relation to civics and democracy. *Critical media literacy* adheres to similar core concepts as ML more generally but with an increased focus on identifying oppressive messages in media and using media to create counternarratives; critical media literacy is inherently tied to "developing skills that will enhance democratization and participation."[18] A study on an intervention aimed at increasing participant awareness of discrimination in the media emphasizes that ML can enable individuals to be more inclusive and active participants in society.[19]

Although there are many points of difference among these studies, each frames ML as an important component of civic life. In this view, an informed citizenry is necessary to a functioning democracy, and building ML skills could be one route to improving interactions with the mass of information crowding our media ecosystem.

ML and Information Quality

With the unfettered access to information that technology now provides, individuals rarely rely on the prescreening of gatekeepers, such as schools and libraries. Although this is beneficial in many ways, it also means that individuals must learn to assess information using their own sets of skills. Researchers often frame ML as a tool to assist participants in understanding the quality of information they encounter, such as identifying degrees of credibility and reliability, misinformation, and disinformation. Based on our sample of literature, this is a common conceptualization of ML in research—most ML-focused research includes a reference to understanding information quality

---

[17] Joseph Kahne, Nam-Jin Lee, and Jessica Timpany Feezell, "Digital Media Literacy Education and Online Civic and Political Participation," *International Journal of Communication*, Vol. 6, 2012.

[18] Douglas Kellner and Jeff Share, "Toward Critical Media Literacy: Core Concepts, Debates, Organizations, and Policy," *Discourse: Studies in the Cultural Politics of Education*, Vol. 26, No. 3, 2005, pp. 372–373.

[19] Maria Ranieri and Francesco Fabbro, "Questioning Discrimination Through Critical Media Literacy: Findings from Seven European Countries," *European Educational Research Journal*, Vol. 15, No. 4, July 1, 2016.

in some way. The common use of this framing means that there are indefinite examples across the literature, indicating its centrality to ML generally.

Some studies focus on the source of information as an indicator of information quality. For instance, one study uses the RADAR (relevance, authority, date, appearance, and reason) technique for evaluating sources—this approach teaches students to evaluate the relevance of information, the authority of its authors, the date of the information, appearance of the presented information, and the reason for publication.[20] Another study addresses evaluating sources through annotated bibliographies.[21] A third study explores whether ML participants "could distinguish poor quality from strong research sources" and identify bias in press articles, among other outcomes.[22]

Other studies frame ML more generally in relation to understanding the truthfulness of information. For instance, one focuses on "how to question and assess the veracity of news texts," while another evaluates the trustworthiness of politically charged online posts.[23] This research could extend to verifying facts; one study explores civic online reasoning, which "encompasses the ability to effectively search for, evaluate, and verify social and political information online."[24]

---

[20] Jane Mandalios, "RADAR: An Approach for Helping Students Evaluate Internet Sources," *Journal of Information Science*, Vol. 39, No. 4, 2013.

[21] Marcia E. Rapchak, Leslie A. Lewis, Julie K. Motyka, and Margaret Balmert, "Information Literacy and Adult Learners: Using Authentic Assessment to Determine Skill Gaps," *Adult Learning*, Vol. 26, No. 4.

[22] Courtney A. Crist, Susan E. Duncan, and Laurie M. Bianchi, "Incorporation of Cross-Disciplinary Teaching and a Wiki Research Project to Engage Undergraduate Students to Develop Information Literacy, Critical Thinking, and Communication Skills," *Journal of Food Science Education*, Vol. 16, No. 3, 2017.

[23] Jennifer Fleming, "What Do Facts Have to Do with It? Exploring Instructional Emphasis in the Stony Brook News Literacy Curriculum," *Journal of Media Literacy Education*, Vol. 7, No. 3, 2015, p. 73; Joseph Kahne and Benjamin Bowyer, "Educating for Democracy in a Partisan Age: Confronting the Challenges of Motivated Reasoning and Misinformation," *American Educational Research Journal*, Vol. 54, No. 1, 2017.

[24] Sarah McGrew, Joel Breakstone, Teresa Ortega, Mark Smith, and Sam Wineburg, "Can Students Evaluate Online Sources? Learning from Assessments of Civic Online Reasoning," *Theory and Research in Social Education*, Vol. 46, No. 2, 2018, p. 168.

Connections Between Different Conceptualizations of Media Literacy

We noted that these groupings are not mutually exclusive. In fact, one can see how they are conceptually interwoven and all trace back to the classic definition of ML: the ability to access, analyze, evaluate, and communicate messages in a wide variety of forms.[25] In this way, these different approaches to framing ML have significant areas of overlap. For instance, identifying economic motivations that drive the construction of media messages also might involve identifying bias and separating credible sources from noncredible ones. Similarly, sorting reliable information from misinformation and disinformation is one of the key tasks inherent in the type of critical news consumption that is required for individuals to become engaged participants of a democracy. However, the slight differences in framing ML ultimately mean that these articles study different types of interventions and employ different measures of their outcomes.

The wide variation in the ways that authors frame ML for their research presents a challenge to cross-study comparison and shapes the way that we present key findings from past literature throughout this chapter. As we discuss research relating to ML interventions, we urge readers to keep in mind the divergent ways in which these studies frame, and ultimately measure, ML outcomes. We will delve deeper into the topic of measures in Chapter Four.

ML Intervention Dimensions and Associations with Truth Decay–Related Competencies

Taking a broad view, extant research suggests that ML interventions are generally associated with improvements in participants' ML-related competencies. This is largely true across different types of participant groups, such as K–12 students, undergraduates, and even families. In fact, a meta-analysis of 51 ML interventions finds an overall positive effect in participant outcomes that do not vary by either participant age

[25] Aufderheide, 1993, pp. 9–10.

or intervention setting.[26] In this section, we describe dimensions of ML interventions and results of studies that examine their effects. We focus on a variety of characteristics, such as the duration of the intervention, the agent facilitating the intervention, the format in which ML education was delivered (e.g., in traditional classrooms or online), and the content of the interventions. Throughout this discussion, we describe gaps in the literature and provide suggestions for further research. In this section, we address findings and insights related to ML interventions; we do not delve into the measures used by each study. We focus on that topic in Chapter Four.

Duration of the ML Intervention

Researchers have found ML interventions of various durations to be associated with positive outcomes. The previously mentioned meta-analysis finds that, across studies, ML interventions that feature more sessions have a larger effect on participant outcomes.[27] However, a broader survey of the literature—both qualitative and quantitative studies—indicates that even brief exposure to an ML intervention might increase participant capacity in ML competencies. For instance, in a series of articles related to ML interventions and the processing of political information, one group of researchers states that brief, public service announcement–style ML lessons of only a few minutes led to changes in participants' reported perceptions of news bias and credibility, and to an increased understanding of the role that citizens play as critical consumers of media.[28]

---

26 Se-Hoon Jeong, Hyunyi Cho, and Yoori Hwang, "Media Literacy Interventions: A Meta-Analytic Review," *Journal of Communication*, Vol. 62, No. 3, 2012. This review includes studies measuring outcomes related to media knowledge, criticism, perceived realism, influence, behavioral beliefs, attitudes, self-efficacy, and behavior.

27 Jeong, Cho, and Hwang, 2012.

28 Emily K. Vraga, Melissa Tully, and Hernando Rojas, "Media Literacy Training Reduces Perception of Bias," *Newspaper Research Journal*, Vol. 30, No. 4, 2009; Emily K. Vraga, Melissa Tully, Heather Akin, and Hernando Rojas, "Modifying Perceptions of Hostility and Credibility of News Coverage of an Environmental Controversy Through Media Literacy," *Journalism: Theory, Practice and Criticism*, Vol. 13, No. 7, 2012; Emily K. Vraga and Melissa Tully, "Media

Other studies also demonstrate the utility of one-shot ML interventions, including those aimed at teachers. In one study, for instance, researchers offered a single-day training to elementary school teachers that imparted lessons of ML theory and offered examples of ML goals, objectives, and activities.[29] The teachers were then asked to complete a media deconstruction task. Teachers who had received the intervention received higher scores than nonintervention teachers. Such studies as these suggest that semester-long courses or extended exposure might not be needed to make some improvements in ML-related competencies. However, to our knowledge, no study has yet definitively compared outcomes of brief, one-shot ML interventions with longer-term interventions. Though the previously mentioned meta-analysis compares duration across ML research, the featured studies vary in their conceptualization of outcomes,[30] and a focused study with a direct comparison would provide more tangible evidence.

Agents Delivering the ML Intervention

We also explored the identity and qualification of the individual agent who delivered the ML intervention to participants in each study. In some cases, experts or trained teachers led ML education efforts; in others, peers, parents, or online portals were the agents of the intervention. The ML meta-analysis reports that the agent delivering the ML intervention did not have an effect on intervention outcomes,[31] but our view of a broader set of literature reveals some compelling evidence that the agent might matter to participant learning. In one study, researchers asked a series of qualitative questions of ninth-grade students who had been randomly assigned to an ML intervention course; students' responses to open-ended questions about the course (e.g., What did

---

Literacy Messages and Hostile Media Perceptions: Processing of Nonpartisan Versus Partisan Political Information," *Mass Communication and Society*, Vol. 18, No. 4, 2015.

[29] Tracy Marie Scull and Janis Beth Kupersmidt, "An Evaluation of a Media Literacy Program Training Workshop for Late Elementary School Teachers," *Journal of Media Literacy Education*, Vol. 2, No. 3, 2011.

[30] Jeong, Cho, and Hwang, 2012.

[31] Jeong, Cho, and Hwang, 2012.

you like about this program?) contained direct references to their perceptions of the teachers who delivered the program, suggesting that the agent might in fact be important to the intervention—though this evidence is far from conclusive.[32]

Some studies are not concerned with the identity of the agent but detail their training. Results on the influence of teacher training on student outcomes, however, are somewhat mixed. In a case demonstrating that ML interventions might improve participant competencies, a study used mothers as the agent for leading ML interventions with their children.[33] They trained participating mothers in ML and related skills and how to use these skills in interactions with their children—for instance, through modeling—particularly when discussing frightening news stories. Children and mothers were then shown a news clip that could be perceived as threatening, and the mothers interacted with their children. The children whose mothers received the ML training prior to those interactions evidenced lower threat perceptions in light of the news story than did those whose mothers did not receive the training. In this case, it appeared that the ML training did help support the children's learning. This would be consistent with the education field more broadly, in which it is often accepted that the training and preparation of the teacher leading a classroom plays an important role in student outcomes.[34]

Other studies, however, appear to show that ML participants might benefit from an intervention regardless of whether their teacher has received explicit ML training. One study trained half of a group of participating teachers in a one-day ML workshop.[35] All the participating teachers then delivered ten lessons of 45–50 minutes to their

---

[32] Brian A. Primack, Danielle Fine, Christopher K. Yang, Dustin Wickett, and Susan Zickmund, "Adolescents' Impressions of Antismoking Media Literacy Education: Qualitative Results from a Randomized Controlled Trial," *Health Education Research*, Vol. 24, No. 4, 2008.

[33] Comer et al., 2008.

[34] Linda Darling-Hammond, "Teacher Quality and Student Achievement," *Education Policy Analysis Archives*, Vol. 8, No. 1, 2000.

[35] Fingar and Jolls, 2013.

classes. The researchers found that participating students demonstrated improved understanding of media issues (such as understanding that media images are often unrealistic and that advertising can affect children's behaviors) regardless of whether their teachers had received the training. This study followed up on student outcomes—one of only a few studies we located that did so—retesting in the following academic year, finding that there was still evidence of the effects of the ML course, though they had decreased. Such studies as this suggest that training of agents might not be as important as one might presume, though more research is needed.

Another study addresses the question of agent affect.[36] Researchers studying seventh- and eighth-grade students separated the students into a control group that received no additional ML lessons and two experimental groups—one of which received a "fact based" ML lesson, presented with limited emotion, while the other received an "affect-added" lesson, in which the presenter used an emotive teaching style. The researchers found that students who received the lessons in both fact-based and affect-added styles showed improvements in ML-related competencies, such as a readiness to ask questions and skepticism regarding media content. In this case, as with the previous study, characteristics of the agents did not appear to be meaningfully related to differences in participant outcomes. Notably, however, there are a large number of intervening and moderating variables not considered in these studies. For example, it is possible that the influence of the agent increases over time, or that agent characteristics matter more for certain types of topics or for certain groups of participants.

Some articles feature nontraditional agents of ML education. For instance, ML interventions in some studies were led by trained peer-group members who delivered ML-related lessons to groups of their peers.[37] Other research assesses the use of online PowerPoint presenta-

---

[36] Austin et al., 2006.

[37] Erica Weintraub Austin, Bruce E. Pinkleton, Yi-Chun Chen, and Bruce W. Austin, "Processing of Sexual Media Messages Improves Due to Media Literacy Effects on Perceived Message Desirability," *Mass Communication and Society*, Vol. 18, No. 4, 2015; Bruce E. Pinkleton, Erica Weintraub Austin, Yi-Chun Chen, and Marilyn Cohen, "Assessing Effects

tions, presumably without human interaction, as a direct method of ML delivery.[38] Although these studies as a group suggest that participants' ML-related competencies might improve following an intervention across a broad variety of types of agents, each study considers very different outcome measures, making direct comparison difficult. Many current ML programs are available directly to participants online, yet we did not find articles comparing the internet as an agent delivering ML education with in-person delivery. For instance, does seeing an ML-related announcement on a social media feed have an influence on these competencies? How does that differ from the influence of an in-person lesson? As the internet provides one possibility for scaling up ML education, this could be an important area for further research.

Finally, other literature shed additional light on agents leading ML education but did not link them to participant outcomes. One study details Swedish teachers' perspectives on ML education, comparing them with those of American teachers,[39] reporting that the Swedish teachers viewed ML as more integrated into other curricula then did American teachers. Future work could consider how the perspective and viewpoints of agents might relate to student outcomes.

Format for Delivery of ML Interventions

In the majority of the studies we reviewed, discrete ML lessons were delivered in what appeared to be traditional class formats, with a teacher as agent and learners in the role of participants. This traditional format of delivery is often taken for granted in the literature, and because it is rarely described in detail, it is difficult to draw conclusions about its relation to participant outcomes. There were, however, several exceptions in which ML was delivered in a nontraditional format;

---

of a Media Literacy–Based Intervention on US Adolescents' Responses to and Interpretations of Sexual Media Messages," *Journal of Children and Media*, Vol. 7, No. 4, 2013.

[38] Vraga, Tully, and Rojas, 2009.

[39] Paul Mihailidis, "Media Literacy in Journalism/Mass Communication Education: Can the United States Learn from Sweden?" *Journalism and Mass Communication Educator*, Vol. 60, No. 4, 2006.

notably, these studies do not compare their alternative format for delivery with a more traditional, stand-alone classroom approach.

Some studies considered ML intervention outcomes under nontraditional course arrangements. In one relatively small study, ML lessons were delivered using a "flipped classroom"—an approach in which classroom time was used to actively engage students in groups rather than to focus on "knowledge delivery," such as lecturing.[40] Students in the flipped classroom improved in the areas of information-processing tasks, among others. This study did not compare outcomes of the flipped classroom with a more traditionally formatted classroom.

In another set of studies, ML interventions occurred in participants' homes. For instance, researchers designed an intervention that was delivered in the format of a computer game that families could engage in together at home.[41] Families in this study used Media Detective Family (MDF), a computer game intended to build ML skills. The researchers did not find statistically significant evidence that use of the computer game improved participants' media deconstruction skills, although this might be because the study was underpowered; the results indicated the intervention was successful in other ways.[42]

Some research approaches ML as integrated with other courses. In one study, researchers used the California Health and English Language Arts standards to undergird lessons, linking ML to existing topics covered in schools.[43] Posttest assessments in this study indicated improvement in student knowledge and beliefs. It is possible, as noted in Chapter Two, that continued exposure to ML in schools would be more realistic if the ML content were linked to existing curricular

---

[40] Siu Cheung Kong, "Developing Information Literacy and Critical Thinking Skills Through Domain Knowledge Learning in Digital Classrooms: An Experience of Practicing Flipped Classroom Strategy," *Computers and Education*, Vol. 78, 2014.

[41] Tracy M. Scull, Janis B. Kupersmidt, and Tara N. Weatherholt, "The Effectiveness of Online, Family-Based Media Literacy Education for Substance Abuse Prevention in Elementary School Children: Study of the Media Detective Family Program," *Journal of Community Psychology*, Vol. 45, No. 6, 2017.

[42] Scull, Kupersmidt, and Weatherholt, 2017.

[43] Fingar and Jolls, 2013.

work, another area in which we think further research would be helpful. Indeed, as already noted, the ML meta-analysis finds that increased exposure is related to increased ML intervention effectiveness.[44]

A key observation emerging from our review of intervention delivery is that many ML studies could benefit from stronger descriptions of how interventions were delivered. There are likely many differences in the formats that are used even in traditional classroom settings, and more nuanced descriptions in the research would benefit a more detailed comparison. We did not see direct comparisons of traditional lesson delivery with other creative formats of lesson delivery, which could shed additional light on the best approach to teaching ML.

Creation as a Central Element of ML Interventions

We found that much of the research we reviewed does not describe the content of ML interventions in great detail. There were some exceptions, however, particularly as related to media creation. As we heard from interviewees, media creation appears to be gaining traction as a central focus of ML education. This might be because understanding the processes of media production can help in identifying the motives, purposes, and points of view embedded in messages.[45] Some studies are designed specifically to assess the impact of media creation as a key component of ML education and a mechanism to teach ML competencies.

In one study, students attended lectures by experts in media and communications and were also assigned a creative task: they created "Wiki research projects" in which they essentially generated a report about a particular kind of food using "high-quality, science-based references."[46] These projects were peer-reviewed by others in the course, and the projects were scored by trained scorers employing a rubric. The authors found that students improved in their ability to critically evalu-

---

[44] Jeong, Cho, and Hwang, 2012.

[45] Renee Hobbs, *Digital and Media Literacy: A Plan of Action. A White Paper on the Digital and Media Literacy Recommendations of the Knight Commission on the Information Needs of Communities in a Democracy*, Washington, D.C.: Aspen Institute, 2010.

[46] Crist et al., 2017, p. 83.

ate and use research through the project. Another study examines an intervention for undergraduate college students taking an ML course.[47] The course focused on how to respond to media through appropriate channels and how to create media content. Using a quasi-experimental design, researchers separated students into two groups, one receiving the creative ML course. They found that the group participating in the course had a more sophisticated understanding of media structures and business models, and more-critical views of advertisers, than those who did not. Yet another project describes how engagement with a student reporting lab influenced participants' communication and technical skills, intellectual curiosity, ability to give and receive feedback, and confidence in self-expression.[48] The reporting lab gave students the ability to play the role of a reporter, which required them to seek out varied opinions, synthesize information, and successfully communicate ideas. This study finds that students who participated in the program had demonstrated growth in specific competency areas, such as communication and technical skills.

These studies are informative but do not offer comparisons between interventions that use creation as a tool and those that adhere to more passive formats of lesson delivery, such as lectures, or those focused on the consumption rather than production sides of ML. We located one study that does treat media creation as an independent variable.[49] These authors found that creating media—in the case of their study, creating antismoking ads—elicited more positive perceptions of the ML intervention than did a similar intervention that did not include an element of creation. In addition, participants in the intervention strengthened their negative perceptions of smoking, a change in attitude that was a key goal of the study.

---

[47] Duran et al., 2008.

[48] Renee Hobbs, "When Teens Create the News: Examining the Impact of PBS News Hour Student Reporting Labs," *Journalism Education*, Vol. 5, No. 1, 2016.

[49] Smita C. Banerjee and Kathryn Greene, "Analysis Versus Production: Adolescent Cognitive and Attitudinal Responses to Antismoking Interventions," *Journal of Communication*, Vol. 56, No. 4, 2006.

New media, such as social media platforms and other online vehicles, allow individuals to be the producers of new information released into the public domain.[50] In such an environment, the creation and sharing of media is likely to become increasingly important and could warrant additional attention in ML literature.

Participant Profiles

We considered whether the kinds of participants receiving ML interventions (whether they were K–12 students, college students, or adults) mattered. As illustrated in the previous sections, many ML studies focus on K–12 or college students. Across these studies, there is evidence that interventions were associated with improvements in participants' ML-related competencies. Because the kinds of interventions and the measured outcomes in this literature are so diverse, we are unable to provide insight regarding the kinds of ML education that are most effective for different participants. However, we identified some gaps in existing knowledge related to participant profiles.

Few studies explicitly addressed outcomes for either very young children or adults who were past their formal educational years. This makes sense, given that students in traditional educational settings might be the most likely to be receiving targeted interventions. There are a few studies that specifically considered ML interventions and outcomes for adults, but these were relatively rare. For instance, one previously mentioned study considers how ML training provided to teachers improves their own ML skills or knowledge.[51] We cannot overstate the importance of adults in the current media ecosystem, and the role they play in the spread of misinformation and disinformation.[52] Addi-

---

[50] Henry Jenkins, "Confronting the Challenges of Participatory Culture: Media Education for the 21st Century (Part One)," *Nordic Journal of Digital Literacy*, Vol. 2, No. 1, 2007; Ioana Literat, "Measuring New Media Literacies: Towards the Development of a Comprehensive Assessment Tool," *Journal of Media Literacy Education*, Vol. 6, No. 1, 2014.

[51] Scull and Kupersmidt, 2012.

[52] See Andrew Guess, Jonathon Nagler, and Joshua Tucker, "Less Than You Think: Prevalence and Predictors of Fake News Dissemination on Facebook," *Science Advances*, Vol. 5, No. 1, 2019.

tional studies regarding how ML interventions could most effectively improve adults' ML-related competencies would be valuable.

There also appears to be a gap in existing literature in the area of marginalized communities and ML education. Although much of the work taking place today in the educational research world is equity-oriented—focused on closing gaps in student achievement—we did not see that as a primary focus across studies of ML. Some studies made a point of engaging a diverse group of participants, but the question of equity was not central to the inquiry. Are all groups influenced equally by exposure to ML education? How does ML reach individuals who have limited access to new forms of media, such as those made possible by the internet? Some experts assert that a gap persists between individuals with the skills to deftly navigate the new information ecosystem and those without them.[53] This is a concern for those interested in equity; individuals without the skills to navigate the digital information system could miss opportunities or lose relative power within a society that increasingly relies on technology for interaction.[54] This is another area for further research.

Limitations of ML Research

Throughout this chapter, we noted some detailed areas in which further research would be useful. There are also some overarching limitations that we must address. Most centrally, the wide variety of outcomes, different measures used to capture those outcomes, and the methods used in this collection of studies presented practical problems in terms of aggregating evidence in a systematic way. This has been previously noted by others who have compiled reviews of ML research.[55] Although

---

[53] Sonia Livingstone and Ellen Helsper, "Gradations in Digital Inclusion: Children, Young People and the Digital Divide," *New Media and Society*, Vol. 9, No. 4, 2007; Alexander Van Deursen and Jan Van Dijk, "Internet Skills and the Digital Divide," *New Media and Society*, Vol. 13, No. 6, 2011.

[54] Sonia Livingstone, "Media Literacy and the Challenge of New Information and Communication Technologies," *Communication Review*, Vol. 7, No. 1, 2004.

[55] Sonia Livingstone and Nancy Thumim, *Assessing the Media Literacy of UK Adults: A Review of the Academic Literature*, London: Broadcasting Standards Commission, Independent Television Commission, and National Institute of Adult Continuing Education, March 2003; David

it is not necessary, or practical, for all studies in a particular field to use the same outcomes or measures, some agreement would make the task of comparing evidence across studies significantly more straightforward. It is difficult to understand how these studies speak to one another across such differences, meaning that our understanding of exactly what works in ML education is in a relatively early stage of development. Because each study captures a different set of outcomes, the evidence does not accumulate to build a generalizable picture of lessons learned from ML studies. Instead, we have series of specific findings relevant to divergent outcomes. They appear to relate, they overlap in many ways, but they do not directly link to one another. Yet multidisciplinary synthesis would be optimal in order for the field to build and develop knowledge that improves ML practice.

Across ML studies, there is also an unevenness in the ways measures are used; in terms of research methodology, we found a limited number of articles that employ causal methods to isolate the effects of ML interventions. We recognize the value of the diversity in research methods used across this literature; qualitative studies offer particularly rich descriptions and compelling findings related to ML education. However, if the question at hand is related to the effectiveness of ML education in improving participant outcomes in particular competencies, the field would also benefit from more concrete evaluative evidence directly attributed to ML programs. In order to make causal arguments about the effect of media literacy programs on student outcomes, the evaluation itself must be designed to isolate the effect of the intervention from other factors that might be related to outcomes of interest. Currently, there is limited evidence of this nature available. One reason for this could be that although program evaluations are often circulated among program creators, funders, or other internal audiences for program improvement, they are not circulated for public knowledge. Another reason could be limited funding for this particu-

Buckingham, Shaku Banaji, Andrew Burn, Diane Carr, Sue Cranmer, and Rebekah Willett, *The Media Literacy of Children and Young People: A Review of the Research Literature on Behalf of Ofcom*, London: Centre for the Study of Children, Youth and Media, 2005.

lar approach to research in ML. This is one area of research in which the ML field would benefit from further work.

Summary

In this chapter, we reviewed existing research across different areas of ML to investigate key questions in our exploration of ML. We first explored how ML was conceptualized by researchers in this field and found three common ways that the collected studies frame ML education. The first of these framings relates to the economic motivations that undergird popular media and information streams. The second type of framing explores ML as related to democracy and civic life. Finally, and most commonly, research frames ML as a way to evaluate the quality of information. We view these three framings as conceptually interdependent, but their differences have implications for comparing results across ML-related research, as the types of outcomes measured correspondingly vary.

We next examined dimensions of ML interventions and explored the degree to which evidence suggests that ML interventions are associated with improvements in ML competencies. We found evidence that ML interventions, as a whole, appear useful in developing the study-specific competencies measured but note that it is difficult to compare across this body of evidence. We remain tentative in our certainty about the relationship between ML interventions and outcomes—especially when we try to identify the specific types of ML interventions that are likely to be effective.

As a result, although we offer this review for background, there are real limitations to the extent to which we can draw definitive conclusions from this research regarding what works in ML interventions. The different outcomes at the center of each study, the variety of measures employed, and some constraints in terms of methodology used all limit the degree to which we can confidently offer suggestions regarding the kinds of ML that are most effective. We continue the conversation around outcomes and measures in ML studies in the next chapter.

CHAPTER FOUR

Measurement and Media Literacy

In Chapter Three, we reviewed literature on dimensions and results of ML interventions. As a whole, the directionality of ML research suggests that interventions likely contribute to growth in relevant participant competencies. However, inconsistencies in the ways that ML competencies were defined and measured limit our confidence in conclusions drawn across this literature. We are not the first to remark on this shortcoming; others who have conducted systematic reviews of ML research in the past have noted similar challenges.[1] Without some commonality, the degree to which evidence can be aggregated across research is limited. Aggregated evidence is important in identifying patterns of what works and what does not; such evidence informs policy, identifies challenges, and guides adjustments in the field. Because of the centrality of this issue to a body of research, we dedicate this chapter to further exploring measures of ML.

There are three factors that we identify as contributing to the variation in outcomes and measures used across ML and related research. First, ML competencies themselves are nuanced and context-specific, making them a challenge to measure. To this point, we describe some key considerations for developing appropriate assessments for hard-to-measure skills, such as those related to ML. Second, the ways that researchers define ML competencies is inconsistent across the literature. We introduce a few examples of ML "standards" in order to highlight

---

[1] Lynda J. Bergsma and Mary E. Carney, "Effectiveness of Health-Promoting Media Literacy Education: A Systematic Review," *Health Education Research*, Vol. 23, No. 3, 2008; Jeong, Cho, and Hwang, 2012.

their complexity and to stress that there is currently not agreement across the field regarding how to define them. Finally, ML research comes from a variety of different disciplines—library sciences, sociology, journalism, public health, and political science, to name a few. These disciplines all have their own traditions in terms of defining and measuring outcomes, and it follows that researchers bring these traditions to the study of ML. We offer examples of different measures employed in ML research and explain some of the strengths and weaknesses inherent in each. We conclude the chapter with summary observations about why developing some concordance in the field—regarding defining ML competencies and their measures—could be beneficial for ML moving forward.

What Makes a Good Measure?

One reason for variation across measures of ML competencies is that they are complex, process-oriented, and context-dependent. In a relevant report, Soland, Hamilton, and Stecher explored options for assessing difficult-to-measure competencies, similar to those associated with ML.[2] They identified three sets of considerations that are relevant when choosing measures: instructional, practical, and technical. Instructional considerations are those related to the educational purpose of a measure. These are less critical when a measure is being used explicitly for research because outcomes will not necessarily be used to inform immediate changes for individual teachers or students. An example of a first-step instructional consideration is whether an assessment is formative (intended to inform ongoing instruction) or summative (assessing growth at the conclusion of a unit). Again, these considerations are more likely relevant to classroom contexts than research contexts, depending on the goals and designs of the research.

A second set of practical considerations is highly relevant to a discussion of ML outcomes. A key tension with measuring ML competencies is that the types of measures that might capture their nuance are

---

[2] Jim Soland, Laura Hamilton, and Brian Stecher, *Measuring 21st Century Competencies: Guidance for Educators*, Santa Monica, Calif.: Asia Society and RAND Corporation, 2013.

also more labor-intensive and expensive to implement. Related practical concerns are the ease of scoring a particular measure, how quickly scorers can be trained at collecting and evaluating necessary data, and other issues of implementation.[3] Another practical consideration is how easy it is to interpret the resulting data; measures that are transparent and easily interpreted can be particularly beneficial when communicating the value of a program or resource to external audiences, such as policymakers or funders, who might have less technical understanding or simply want straightforward results in light of their overburdened schedules. Ease of interpretation must be weighed against the need for complex skills to be assessed by more complex measures in order to better tease out their nuances.[4]

As is clear from these considerations, there is often a difficult balance between the need for complexity and realistic constraints on time and other resources. For example, multiple-choice measures might be simpler to administer, but these often provide less-nuanced information than would be supplied by a more intricate, applied assessment task that requires a time-intensive scoring and interpretation process. Some in the ML community have warned that the temptation to use simplistic measures carries the risk of influencing how we actually define the multifaceted competencies linked to ML education. If the practical constraints of a measure overshadow construct validity—how the measure relates to core theoretical concepts—there is a risk that research could begin to actually frame those concepts in oversimplified ways.[5] One approach to ameliorate tension between practical constraints and complexity is to rely on a standard set of core measures while also allowing for specialized supplemental measures.[6] This can

---

[3] Soland, Hamilton, and Stecher, 2013.

[4] Soland, Hamilton, and Stecher, 2013.

[5] Monica E. Bulger, "Measuring Media Literacy in a National Context: Challenges of Definition, Method and Implementation," *Media Studies*, Vol. 3, No. 6, 2012.

[6] National Research Council, "Indicators," *The Importance of Common Metrics for Advancing Social Science Theory and Research: A Workshop Summary*, Washington, D.C.: National Academies Press, 2011.

provide a degree of flexibility and an ability to update a set of measures over time or as a program or context evolves and changes.

Finally, there are technical considerations that Soland, Hamilton, and Stecher outline: validity, reliability, and fairness. They refer to validity as the "extent to which there is evidence to support specific interpretations of test scores for specific uses or purposes."[7] *Construct validity*, for instance, assesses the extent to which a measure actually captures what it is intended to measure.[8] For example, if a primary objective of an ML intervention is for participants to be able to assess online source credibility, then a measure should evaluate just that. But it is common for current measures to address attitudes and knowledge rather than changes in competency.[9] As we discuss later, some measures in the literature today instead ask individuals how confident they are in their ability to assess sources or to explain how they can tell whether a source is credible; these approaches approximate the focal competency and could be useful for understanding participant thinking, but they do not determine actual growth in the competency itself. This is a challenge not only in research; assessments available to the interested public and to educators are also often a poor fit for ML competencies. A recent article in which the authors surveyed digital literacy assessments observes that, "Unfortunately, assessments of students' abilities to evaluate online information are in short supply. Many digital literacy lesson plans are accompanied by short assessments. These assessments often take the form of multiple-choice or short-answer questions that focus on rote knowledge or on what students say they would do in hypothetical situations."[10]

Reliability is another technical consideration relevant to the selection of measures. There are several forms of reliability—one of which,

---

[7] Soland, Hamilton, and Stecher, 2013, p. 13.

[8] There are several ways to consider validity from a research perspective. For instance, *face validity* refers to the extent to which a measure tests what it aims to test, *predictive validity* refers to the ability of one measure to predict later performance, and *construct validity* assesses the extent to which a measure relates to the underlying theoretical concepts.

[9] Bergsma and Carney, 2008.

[10] McGrew et al., 2018, p. 169.

known as *test-retest reliability*, measures the extent to which a participant who takes an assessment more than once under similar conditions will get similar scores at each testing point.[11] A large difference across these two tests, without an intervention in the interim, would suggest that the test is not reliable. ML competencies are inherently difficult to assess reliably because they are rooted in the idea of interpretation; how people understand media messages is a result of their own backgrounds and other contextual factors. In the following discussion of ML measures, we keep in mind the ways that individuals' interpretations (educators and participants alike) can have implications for reliability.

Finally, fairness is a crucial consideration that Soland, Hamilton, and Stecher describe. If measures of ML outcomes are to be of value in informing a widespread effort to build societal resilience to Truth Decay, they must measure constructs that are not dependent on participants' belonging to any particular group (e.g., ethnicity, native language, or socioeconomic status). When assessing digital competencies, as might be expected in measures of some ML skills, one could imagine that the "digital divide" could introduce vital questions about the fairness of an assessment.[12] ML employed as a tool to counter Truth Decay would require an increase in ML competencies for all, meaning that it is critically important to understand outcomes across all demographic, economic, educational, and other boundaries.

These considerations are central to a conversation about ML measures. Many of the guidelines for developing appropriate measures hinge on the ways that outcomes are defined. Therefore, we next provide some examples of ML standards to better orient the conversation on measures.

---

[11] There are multiple ways to conceptualize reliability in assessment. For instance, *internal reliability* refers to the consistency of scores across many items designed to capture a single construct. *Inter-rater reliability* pertains to the consistency of scores, as assigned by more than one rater, for the same item in the same context.

[12] For considerations regarding the digital divide, see Livingstone and Helsper, 2007.

What Should We Measure?

There is little agreement around the specific skills encompassed by ML education—in fact, there is divergence in the field about whether ML should be viewed in sets of discrete skills at all or conceptualized more holistically. Because we are interested in research related to ML effectiveness, we contend that defining explicit competencies is a key step to developing appropriate measures and necessary for research regarding ML intervention effectiveness. In education, focal competencies are often written as *standards*; to measure what matters, we first name and define the thing to be measured. Then, assessments can be developed that are fitting to those standards, and instruction can be aligned to them.[13] The ways that specific competencies are defined matters for the ways that they are assessed.

We provide a set of ML competencies in Table 4.1 for explanatory purposes. We offer these to (1) illustrate for readers the kinds of complex competencies we are referring to as we offer examples of measures in the second half of this chapter, and (2) highlight the variety of different disciplines in which ML-related competencies exist. We compiled this list throughout our data collection processes. These consisted of discussing ML with experts, reviewing extant literature, and developing an inventory of active ML programs. We reviewed existing sets of standards, competencies, and skills from a wide variety of sources identified in these processes, then selected examples that are both central to ML and likely to be relevant in efforts to counter Truth Decay. The sets of standards that we reviewed were not drawn strictly from ML literature. Some of those we selected were from information literacy; some were digital-literacy based. To interviewees' point in Chapter One that integrating ML skills across core content areas appears feasible today, two of the standards we selected are borrowed from Common Core

[13] See Marshall Smith and Jennifer O'Day, "Systemic School Reform," in Susan Fuhrman and Betty Malen, eds., *The Politics of Curriculum and Testing: The 1990 Yearbook of the Politics of Education Association*, New York: Falmer Press, 1991; and Andrew C. Porter, "Measuring the Content of Instruction: Uses in Research and Practice," *Educational Researcher*, Vol. 31, No. 7, 2002.

Table 4.1
Selected Media Literacy-Related Competencies Relevant to Mitigating Truth Decay

Standards
1. Recognize the demand for and be able to search for, access, and retrieve information and media content.[a]
2. Use evidence to investigate questions; devise and implement a plan to fill knowledge gaps.[b]
3. Analyze information from multiple sources and identify complexities, discrepancies, and different perspectives.[c]
4. Evaluate characteristics of information products that indicate the underlying creation processes.[d]
5. Trace and evaluate an argument and specific claims in a text, assessing whether the reasoning is sound and the evidence is relevant and sufficient to support the claims.[e]
6. Students create original works or responsibly repurpose or remix digital resources into new creations.[f]
7. Communicate discoveries in ways that suit the purpose and audience.[g]

[a] UNESCO, 2013.

[b] American Association of School Librarians, *AASL Standards Framework for Learners: National School Library Standards for Learners, School Librarians, and School Libraries*, Chicago, Ill., 2018.

[c] California Department of Education, *Model School Library Standards for California Public Schools*, Sacramento, Calif., 2011.

[d] Association of College and Research Libraries, *Information Literacy Competency Standards for Higher Education*, Chicago, Ill.: American Library Association, 2000.

[e] National Governors Association Center for Best Practices, Council of Chief State School Officers, 2010.

[f] International Society of Technology in Education, undated.

[g] National Council of Teachers of English, "NCTE/IRA Standards for the English Language Arts," webpage, undated.

NOTE: The exact wording of these standards has been slightly modified in some cases to better fit the format of this report.

State Standards. The standards in Table 4.1 suggest the types of ML outcomes that might be measured for a particular age group.[14]

As written, several of these standards require further parsing to make them appropriate for measurement. For instance, the standard "Trace and evaluate an argument and specific claims in a text, assessing

[14] ML standards should be written and interpreted differently depending on audience; we generated this list considering students at approximately a high school level and above, but ML should not be limited to older participants—these skills could be adapted for younger grades or different developmental stages.

whether the reasoning is sound and the evidence is relevant and sufficient to support the claims" could be broken into several discrete competencies used to drive the development of measures, such as "assess whether the reasoning is sound" and "assess whether the evidence is relevant to support the claims"—each of which could be challenging to measure in its own right. UNESCO's set of media and information literacy competencies does just that, breaking down the standard "Recognize the demand for, be able to search for, be able to access and retrieve information and media content" into smaller components.[15]

We do not offer this list as a suggested set of ML standards for moving forward but to emphasize the kinds of complex competencies involved with ML education. Many of them are process-oriented and could be applied in diverse contexts and subject areas; for instance, one could "analyze information from multiple sources" in many settings and for different purposes. This could be done in a discrete ML course or in science, history, language arts, or other core academic courses. Process-oriented competencies differ from those that are content-focused, which are inextricably linked to a subject area (e.g., learning about a particular historical event or the periodic table). Notably, the complexity of these different competencies increases the measurement challenge associated with them, which is worth keeping in mind as we focus on measures in the next section.

The standards in Table 4.1 also highlight the variety of places where ML-related standards can be found. These standards were collected from a variety of sources and disciplines, which is notable because there are many overlapping standards or competencies across them. Although it is not necessary or probable that a single agreed-upon set of ML standards could be shared across all related disciplines, there could be some advantages to deciding on a set of common standards where notable overlap exists. This would allow for ML research and evaluations to build on each other over time, leading to a more robust set of evidence to learn from.

---

[15] UNESCO, 2013.

What Kinds of Measures Are Most Useful for ML Research?

In this section, we describe seven types of measures we identified in ML and related studies: self-report measures, multiple-choice measures, task-based measures, innovative computer-based assessments, portfolio assessments, real-life observations, and large-scale online data collection. In discussing each type of measure, we offer a description, provide an example of the measure's use in extant research, and highlight some of its strengths and weaknesses in light of our discussion. We intend for this section to provide a way of thinking about the options for ML measurement by identifying and summarizing benefits and drawbacks of each option.

This list is not exhaustive. Our review also is not reflective of the proportionality of measure types used in ML-related studies today. Some types appear more common than others; self-reports, for instance, are more prevalent in the literature than are portfolio assessments. Because they might be useful for measuring the complex types of competencies at the core of ML education, we draw attention to some of the less common types of measures used in ML research—such as observations—in addition to those that are widespread. We also note that these measures are not mutually exclusive; a computer assessment also might be task-based, for example. In this section, we focus on the format that the measures take but note that there is also variation in the rigor of the design and application of these measures—another potential topic for future research.

Self-Report Measures in ML Research

In our review of the literature, we found several studies that relied on self-reporting in their measures of outcomes. Self-reporting allows respondents to rate or judge their own abilities, as opposed to demonstrating their competency with tasks or skill-based questions or observing actual changes in behavior. Self-report items are typically based on a Likert scale and administered in the form of a survey or questionnaire. Although there are numerous ML studies in our sample that employ self-report measures, they rarely rely on the same instrument. Some examples of self-report items are as follows:

- I am confident in my ability to personalize the information I receive through online news sites.[16]
- I generally compare different websites to decide if information is true.[17]
- I know how to use a wide range of strategies when searching for information.[18]
- I am able to enter the right words in a search engine to find what I am looking for.[19]

In responding to these prompts, participants answered on Likert scales, denoting their degree of confidence in a particular competency. In cases in which the goal was to understand participant outcomes as related to self-efficacy, these kinds of self-report measures were well suited to the inquiry. That was the case in some studies; for instance, Scull and Kupersmidt researched teachers who attended a one-day ML training.[20] Before and after the training, they asked the teachers questions about the importance of ML and their familiarity with it. The researchers were interested in teacher self-efficacy, so these measures were relevant. The researchers also measured changes in the teachers' scores on a media deconstruction task to evaluate actual growth in competencies.

Many of the benefits of self-reporting are related to practical considerations. For instance, self-report measures are efficient; they typi-

---

[16] Tom Hallaq, "Evaluating Online Media Literacy in Higher Education: Validity and Reliability of the Digital Online Media Literacy Assessment (DOMLA)," *Journal of Media Literacy Education*, Vol. 8, No. 1, 2016, p. 75.

[17] Alexander Van Deursen, Ellen Johanna Helsper, and Rebecca Eynon, *Measuring Digital Skills: From Digital Skills to Tangible Outcomes Project Report*, London: London School of Economics, University of Twente, and Oxford Internet Institute, 2014, p. 14.

[18] Van Deursen, Helsper, and Eynon, 2014.

[19] Literat, 2014, p. 27.

[20] Scull and Kupersmidt, 2011.

cally do not require an investment in developing a scoring protocol or rubric or in training scorers, and these measures can be automatically scored using a variety of technological methods. They might be particularly attractive in the case of ML, in which the competencies themselves are a challenge to measure in other, more-applied ways. Depending on the study and conceptualization of outcomes, relying on participant self-reporting might be appropriate and useful—for instance, if a study is intended to assess participant self-efficacy. Though self-reporting might be sufficient for this use, this approach is not effective for demonstrating growth in actual ML competencies; exclusively measuring individual perceptions does not address whether or how ML education builds participant capacity.

There are significant, well-documented drawbacks to relying on self-reporting. Misinterpreted as objective assessments, self-report measures can lead readers to conclusions that are not actually supported by the data; a measure that asks participants to rate their own competency in evaluating sources should not be interpreted as an accurate assessment of actual competency in that area. Additionally, self-report measures are susceptible to social desirability bias; for instance, a student might provide the response they believe their teachers want to see. In addition, not all groups are equally reliable as self-reporters. Previous research has shown that adolescents in particular are prone to providing incorrect responses, for a variety of reasons, when reporting on their own behavior or competencies.[21] This is problematic for studies of ML, which often use school-aged populations as test subjects. Self-reporting is also vulnerable to biases of social identity. In other words, respondents might answer a question in a way that does not reflect their actual perceptions, but instead how they feel individuals within the group they belong to should answer. Finally, individuals' responses might vary greatly over time simply because their own perspectives change. As a person becomes more literate in an area, they could become increasingly aware of what they do not know, leading to

---

[21] Xitao Fan, Brent C. Miller, Kyung-Eun Park, Bryan W. Winward, Mathew Christensen, Harold D. Grotevant, and Robert H. Tai, "An Exploratory Study About Inaccuracy and Invalidity in Adolescent Self-Report Surveys," *Field Methods*, Vol. 18, No. 3, 2006, pp. 239–241.

lower self-efficacy ratings after exposure to an intervention. For these reasons, self-report measures are often considered less desirable than other forms of assessment.

Multiple-Choice Assessments of ML and Related Competencies

Multiple-choice measures are a common testing format in ML and other fields. The format prompts participants to choose answers to closed-ended questions from a selection of predesignated options. This has been the traditional format for standardized assessments in the United States in the past, though traditional multiple-choice testing is being displaced in some ways by more-adaptive computerized formats, as we will discuss later. First, we explain one instance of multiple-choice measures used in the field of news literacy and briefly describe some of the advantages and disadvantages of this format.

One study measuring news-focused ML described the processes used for developing and administering a survey.[22] The research team designed a survey around Potter's cognitive model of ML, as applied to news media literacy.[23] As the authors explained it, "Potter's model suggests that media literate individuals think deeply about their media experience, believe they are in control of media's influence, and have a high degree of basic knowledge about media content, industries, and effects."[24] The researchers generated survey items grouped into thematic clusters, including a category of questions designed to gauge participants' knowledge of media structures. They developed multiple-choice questions related to the institutions that produce the news, ways that the news is produced, and what they call the possible effects of news content. These were multiple-choice, closed-ended questions that they asserted each had only one correct answer. The following are examples of these questions:

- Media outlets in the United States are:
  - for-profit businesses

---

22 Maksl et al., 2017.

23 James W. Potter, *Theory of Media Literacy: A Cognitive Approach*, Thousand Oaks, Calif.: SAGE, 2014.

24 Maksl et al., 2017, p. 233.

  - owned by the government
  - nonprofit businesses
  - I don't know
- Which of the following news outlets does NOT depend primarily on advertising for financial support?
  - CNN
  - PBS
  - *The New York Times*
  - *Newsweek* magazine
  - Don't know[25]

There are advantages to using multiple-choice assessments. First, many of the same benefits of self-report measures apply: These assessments can be cost-effective, they are simple to score, and they are scalable. Data from multiple-choice measures can be generalizable and straightforward to compare—across programs, locations, or rounds of administration. In addition, composite measures (including multiple-choice) might be better predictors of media-related literacy competencies than self-reporting alone. [26]

However, there are several challenges associated with employing multiple-choice measures on their own. Almost by definition—given that answer options are predesignated—these assessments cannot effectively take context into consideration. Competencies related to ML are highly dependent on context. Similarly, multiple-choice questions are not designed to measure complex, process-oriented competencies, such as those related to ML. There is a risk in oversimplifying nuanced ML skills to fit such a basic format as multiple-choice; because instruction is often designed with assessment outcomes in mind, measuring ML competencies in a multiple-choice format could lead to offering instruction only in the matched, oversimplified skills.

Multiple-choice measures also bring fairness into question. Answer options are limited to those provided by test designers and are therefore not reflective of the innumerous actual choices an indi-

---

[25] Maksl et al., 2017, p. 241.

[26] Eszter Hargittai, "Survey Measures of Web-Oriented Digital Literacy," *Social Science Computer Review*, Vol. 23, No. 3, 2005.

vidual is presented with while engaged with the information ecosystem in real life. The content of questions might be relevant to the lives of some participants and not others, leading to engagement opportunities that are better for one participant than another. And finally, the lack of flexibility offered by predesignated answers in multiple-choice measures has the potential to ingrain assessment writers' personal or cultural biases in the assessment items. Although these risks might be particularly high because of the closed-ended nature of multiple-choice questions, we recognize that similar biases are also a risk in each of the approaches we describe in this section.

Computer-Based Assessments

Standardized tests are evolving. Far from bubbling in circles using a #2 pencil, many assessments today are administered via computer or tablet. These tests often employ an adaptive format, adjusting the level of difficulty based on test-takers' responses as the assessment progresses. Tests traditionally administered in a multiple-choice format have been moving in a new direction in other ways, as well; they now often allow students to highlight text, move objects from one location to another on a screen, or complete mini-simulations to assess problem-solving skills. It appears that computer-based assessments are not widely used in studying ML competencies, but we did find some examples. In particular, we look at the example of the iSkills assessment, an online assessment of information literacy competencies developed by the Educational Testing Service (ETS). We describe this example of a computer-based assessment, then address some of the strengths and weaknesses of this format more generally.

In the early 2000s, ETS partnered with a cohort of universities to develop the iSkills assessment. The assessment was designed with attention to the nuances of measuring information literacy outcomes—the test developers did not set out to assess discrete skills; rather, they were seeking to examine more holistic knowledge in the context of the digital environment.[27] They considered how the digital environment

[27] Irvin R. Katz, "Testing Information Literacy in Digital Environments: ETS's iSkills Assessment," *Information Technology and Libraries*, Vol. 26, No. 3, 2007.

might mediate the constructs of information literacy that they sought to measure and conducted checks for measure validity.[28] The iSkills assessment was not designed to capture outcomes of a particular intervention, but it could be applied in such a way.

The iSkills developed into a set of online, scenario-based tasks. "Each interactive task presents a real-world scenario, such as a class or work assignment, that frames the information problem. Students solve information-handling tasks in the context of simulated software (for example, e-mail, Web browser, library database) having the look and feel of typical applications."[29] In other words, participants would work through the motions of completing a task in the context of an online platform that emulates the actual information environment. A key characteristic of these particular tasks is that they are not completed by selecting one "correct" answer. Instead, a participant taking the iSkills would need to complete a series of steps in a process; for instance, if participants were told to search for an item, they might need to use a search engine and enter well-selected search terms, all while considering the purpose of the task.[30]

Innovative assessments using newer technology, such as iSkills, have many advantages. Indeed, many high-stakes assessments in education today use a computer-based format even if they are not regularly simulation-based, as iSkills is. One of the benefits of using a computer-based approach is that the assessment itself is easily scaled; an ML test could be administered across numerous ML programs and, if well-designed, provide results for targeted improvement and comparisons between interventions. These assessments take little time to score, and, in some cases, results can be available almost immediately. Additionally, perhaps because of our familiarity with standardized testing in the

---

[28] Irvin R. Katz and Norbert Elliot, "Information Literacy in Digital Environments: Construct Mediation, Construct Modeling, and Validation Processes," in Barbara J. D'Angelo, Sandra Jamieson, Barry Maid, and Janice R. Walker, eds., *Information Literacy: Research and Collaboration Across Disciplines*, Fort Collins, Colo.: WAC Clearinghouse and University Press of Colorado, 2016.

[29] Katz, 2007.

[30] Katz and Elliot, 2016, p. 94.

United States, outcomes of these tests appear to be easy for the general public to interpret. As we noted early in this chapter, results that are easy to interpret can make them more accessible to decisionmakers and practitioners who might not be familiar with research.

Other benefits of using technology for the assessment of ML intervention outcomes relate to the online environment as a mediator of assessment. Much of our interaction with the information ecosystem today is enabled via technological tools. Using the same format to assess outcomes allows a measure to more closely match the competency; if we are interested in understanding how individuals obtain information online, it might be more fitting to assess them using an online format than via paper and pencil.

There are limitations to these assessments, even as technology has evolved and allowed them to become more dynamic. The example we offered, iSkills, requires that participants interact in a simulation of the online environment, requiring completion of several steps to finish a task. For instance, searching a topic online requires multiple steps. This is more realistic than most of the measures we reviewed in the literature related to ML measurement. Assessing a series of processes (as opposed to assessing single competencies in single items) might make it difficult to isolate which specific competencies are problematic for a participant. However, if we take a skill-based approach rather than the holistic one, it could still be a challenge to assess complex competencies, such as synthesizing information and evaluating claims.[31] Finally, technology as a mediator could bring fairness into question because some participants might not be familiar with using computers; it is possible that unfamiliarity with the medium would affect outcomes if a participant could have been successful in a particular competency if it had been evaluated using a method more familiar to the user.

There are several testing organizations currently invested in improving the assessment of difficult-to-measure competencies using technology, which could lead to continued advancements (e.g., ETS, Smarter Balanced, and the Partnership for Assessment of Readiness

---

[31] David Conley, "A New Era for Educational Assessment," *Education Policy Analysis Archives*, Vol. 23, No. 8, 2015.

for College and Careers). Continued developments make it possible to consider more-widespread evaluation of ML outcomes using computerized assessments in future research.

A Task-Based Approach to Assessing ML Competencies

What we are calling *task-based measures* are often referred to as *performance assessments*. This approach offers discrete tasks for a participant to master as scored on a consistent evaluative tool, such as a rubric. A task might mimic a real-life scenario that a participant could encounter, such as watching a news clip or reading an article, and prompt the participant to describe his or her response to the example, such as deconstructing economic motivations of the source or explaining the sufficiency of evidence presented for a claim. Then, trained scorers employ a rubric to assess participants' responses. We came across several examples of task-based assessments in ML literature; we highlight one that was particularly well articulated and discuss strengths and weaknesses of a task-based approach.

In one example of task-based measures, McGrew et al. described the development of a series of task-based assessments to gauge *civic online reasoning*,[32] which is "the ability to judge the credibility of the information that floods young people's smartphones, tablets, and computer screens,"[33] and "the ability to effectively search for, evaluate, and verify social and political information online."[34] The developed assessments were built around three questions that the group calls *core competencies*: (1) Who is behind the information? (2) What is the evidence? and (3) What do other sources say?

The developed tasks were of varied lengths and degrees of complexity, designed for middle-school to college students. The authors offered

[32] Authors of this study are affiliated with the Stanford History Education Group, a research group based out of Stanford University that works with schools and provides free curricula and materials. The group's website hosts a series of task-based assessments available to the public. Stanford History Education Group, homepage, undated.

[33] Sam Wineburg, Sarah McGrew, Joel Breakstone, and Teresa Ortega, *Evaluating Information: The Cornerstone of Civic Online Reasoning*, Stanford, Calif.: Stanford Digital Repository, Stanford University, 2016, p. 3.

[34] McGrew et al., 2018, p. 165.

several examples of the tasks. In one, students were given an article on the topic of the money habits of millennials; the author's byline states that he is an executive at a large national bank.[35] The directions for students read, "Examine the document below and answer the question that follows," followed by, "This article argues that many millennials (people in their mid-20s to mid-30s) need help with financial planning. What is one reason you might not trust this article?" Student responses were scored using the team's developed rubric.

There are several benefits to using task-based assessments in the mold of this example. Notably, they simulate an actual application of participants' comprehension and use of ML skills, which is a different approach from a self-report or a basic multiple-choice assessment. In this way, these assessments are well-suited to assess ML competencies in context, which was a key emphasis of interviewees when it came to thinking about what a "good" ML assessment would look like. Results might more closely reflect participants' actual abilities, as opposed to their perceptions of and beliefs about their abilities. In addition, tasks can be adaptable to contextual needs; generic tasks might be designed to apply to a variety of examples. For instance, the objective of one task could be to assess the reliability of a website, but this task could be designed for use on different websites at an instructor or researcher's discretion—an instructor could ask participants to evaluate purportedly science-based websites, news websites, and others that appear on the surface to be impartial but might actually show evidence of bias once participants begin to explore. Many K–12 schools and universities are equipped with technology that could support these tasks, though a task-based approach would be operable without extensive technological support. Depending on the task, it would be possible (although not ideal) to conduct a task-based assessment with no access to technology whatsoever. For example, participants could complete a task using a physical newspaper as their source.

There are also disadvantages associated with a task-based approach. First, the time required to score task products is nontrivial—particularly if we are considering its use in large-scale research projects.

---

[35] McGrew et al., 2018, p. 174.

Second, although well-designed rubrics and rigorous scorer training typically meet accepted agreement thresholds, rubrics remain reliant on perceptions and might be affected by individual biases. One approach to ameliorate this challenge would be to employ multiple scorers to assess a product based on the same rubric—though this would increase the time and cost burden of this approach—or to administer multiple tasks for one focal skill. Third, reliability challenges stem not from only rater differences but also task sampling. It is generally true that one would need a large number of tasks to produce an overall score with acceptable reliability.[36] Finally, the time requirements and reliability issues lead us to question the scalability of employing task-based measures in research. Thinking toward the future, one expert we interviewed mentioned the possibility of using technology to systematically assess qualitative responses to task-based assessments, but we did not see evidence of that approach in the current literature.

Portfolio Assessments of ML Competencies

Another way to assess ML competencies is through portfolio measures. A portfolio is an approach to assessment that collects artifacts related to the learning process, such as reflections on and actual products of research. Rather than collecting artifacts in a physical portfolio in "real life," some educators use electronic portfolios (e-portfolios) to assess learning. This approach to assessment employs an online platform on which participants store artifacts over time (throughout a semester, year, or totality of time in a program or school). In some cases, participants upload articles that they plan to use in a research project, or they can respond on the portfolio platform to such prompts as, "Write the online search statements that you tried in the lines below. Put a star next to the most useful search statements."[37] Although portfolio assessment was uncommon in the literature we reviewed, it has emerged

---

[36] Reliability, though, is a challenge to assessing ML competencies more generally; central ML concepts are rooted in individuals' interpretations and are influenced by contextual factors, meaning variation is inherent to the constructs.

[37] See Dorothy Anne Warner, "Programmatic Assessment: Turning Process into Practice by Teaching for Learning," *Journal of Academic Librarianship*, Vol. 29, No. 3, 2003, p. 171.

as an important practice for undergraduate education because of its utility for assessing learning in cases for which standardized measurement is not feasible.[38] We describe an example from an information literacy study and explain benefits and limitations of this approach more broadly.

Scharf et al. wrote that they used portfolio assessments to measure information literacy competencies because the authors viewed these assessments as more authentic than other approaches.[39] Portfolios in this study were not used to measure outcomes of any intervention; rather, the researchers were interested in better understanding the portfolio measure itself. The authors applied tenets of information literacy to a set of college students' writing portfolios. The researchers scored final papers in these portfolios using dimensions based on the information literacy standards of the Association of College and Research Libraries. The researchers titled these dimensions—citation, evidence of independent research, appropriateness, integration, and overall information literacy portfolio score[40]—and held trainings during which scorers calibrated their ratings before they graded each portfolio.

Generally, the portfolio approach is valuable if the central skills to be assessed are complex and process-oriented, as ML competencies are. Portfolios provide a central location for a variety of evidence types to be collected—not simply the product of an assignment, but artifacts of the process collected over a period of time. In that way, portfolio assessments are a more authentic form of assessment of process-oriented competencies, such as the ability to determine source credibility. Using a portfolio allows for a clear link between learning and the real world; a participant would not be considering

---

38 The American Association of Colleges and Universities has included e-portfolios among its High Impact Practices. American Association of Colleges and Universities, "ePortfolios," webpage, undated.

39 Davida Scharf, Norbert Elliot, Heather Huey, Vladimir Briller, and Kamal Joshi, "Direct Assessment of Information Literacy Using Writing Portfolios," *Journal of Academic Librarianship*, Vol. 33, No. 4, 2007.

40 Scharf et al., 2007, pp. 462–463.

hypothetical ways in which they might use newly acquired ML skills but rather would have the opportunity to actually apply them. In addition, portfolios can be flexible, applicable across a wide variety of content areas, and able to store information on multiple different kinds of competencies. That is not to say that this approach is ideal. In fact, the labor burden of scoring or evaluating a portfolio is one of its key drawbacks.

Compiling and evaluating portfolios can be time-consuming. To sift through and score a set of artifacts for every participant might not be practical for researchers interested in assessing at a large scale, or for teachers working with dozens of students. Although the time-consuming nature of portfolio assessment could be lessened by online platforms designed to help organize content—and, potentially, by such innovations as machine-learning-based software for automating some of the process—time remains a legitimate practical constraint. In addition, ways in which portfolios are scored or evaluated can vary greatly; clear expectations would need to be set and training adhered to in order to have confidence in results, as is the case with other measures in which a rubric or scoring protocol is employed. Relatedly, a central concern regarding portfolios used for research purposes is the difficulty of gauging their reliability and validity, though there have been some attempts to do so.[41]

Portfolios have particular value for research assessing change over time, such as through pre- and post-assessments or comparisons with control groups. If our interest were in understanding nuanced case studies of ML interventions, portfolios would be one way to accomplish this.

An In-Person Observational Approach to Measuring ML-Related Competencies

The most authentic measure of whether an ML intervention contributed to changed competencies might be found in observational data about how a person interfaces with media in everyday life. Observational measures can be constructed in many different ways; at its core,

[41] Scharf et al., 2007.

an observational measure involves watching the behaviors of participants and using a scoring guide to determine their level of mastery in the focal competencies. A common example of observational measures is those often employed in teacher evaluation practices. In these observations, there is a predetermined rubric that a principal or other trained observer fills out while watching a teacher engage in a lesson. We did not find many examples of observational measures in the ML literature reviewed, though we will describe one example. We then review some of the benefits and limitations of an observational approach to measuring ML outcomes.

One digital literacy study used observations in combination with other forms of data to measure participants' assessment of the credibility of online information.[42] Their study did not measure outcomes of an intervention, but the observation procedure could be applied. In this study, researchers sat next to a participant at a computer and read prompts that would trigger different web-based searches by the participant. For instance, one prompt was, "You are trying to figure out how to write a resume for a summer internship. Find an authoritative source on the subject that helps you identify four key things that need to be on the front page of your resume."[43] The researchers asked participants to think out loud, narrating what they were doing. The researchers made audio recordings that were transcribed, in addition to recording screen shots of the computer monitors participants used, and then analyzed participants' processes through the collected data. If using observations to assess the outcomes of an ML intervention, scorers would need to be trained in an explicit rubric or coding protocol that could be used across participants to document degrees of competency.

In-person observations such as those conducted by Hargittai et al. are beneficial in that they closely mimic real-life scenarios in which participants use technology. Observations provide a better picture of participant competencies than a survey can. In particular, asking par-

---

[42] Eszter Hargittai, Lindsay Fullerton, Ericka Menchen-Trevino, and Kristin Yates Thomas, "Trust Online: Young Adults' Evaluation of Web Content," *International Journal of Communication*, Vol. 4, 2010.

[43] Hargittai et al., 2010, p. 489.

ticipants to narrate their thinking as they complete an information-related task would provide some insight into the processes behind their decisions; this is particularly useful when considering ML competencies, which are often process-oriented. However, the investment of time necessary to use such measures would be costly to employ at scale. In addition, as is the case with other types of measures that use rubrics or scoring guides, reliability of scoring would be a challenge. Another limitation of in-person observations would be the mediating role of the observers themselves. The Hawthorne effect—the problem that individuals might change their behavior because of the knowledge that they are being observed—suggests that participants adopt some degree of performance in their activity because they know that they are being watched.[44]

Using Large-Scale Online Activity Data to Measure Interactions

Today, observational measures are not limited to in-person sessions. Given that much of our interaction with the information ecosystem occurs via technology, we each leave a digital trail. It is therefore possible to track and analyze actual online activities in the aggregate. There are websites that researchers can use to access large sets of data about behaviors of the public—such as the number of times a particular article was shared—and there are ways that researchers could design their own data collection instruments for similar purposes, such as an application that monitors smartphone activity. In recent years, there appears to have been an increase in media-related studies that use these large sets of online activity data; likely, these are motivated by the same concerns that spurred RAND's interest in Truth Decay, such as an uptick in shared misinformation and disinformation on the internet.

We offer two examples of studies using actual online activity to understand media-related trends, though we note that these studies were not designed to address any specific competencies or evaluate ML interventions. First, participants in one study provided researchers

---

[44] For considerations related to the Hawthorne effect, see John G. Adair, "The Hawthorne Effect: A Reconsideration of the Methodological Artifact," *Journal of Applied Psychology*, Vol. 69, No. 2, 1984.

access to their Facebook accounts, which the authors then analyzed for sharing activity,[45] particularly the degree to which participants shared "fake news" articles during the period leading up to the 2016 election. The authors found that there was a strong age effect, with participants over the age of 65 sharing notably more articles from "fake news" domains than other age groups. In this study, the authors note that there are some limitations to the data—for example, participants could have deleted shared articles at some point before giving the researchers access to their accounts. In another study, researchers tracked the circulation of "fake news" since the 2016 election,[46] identifying lists of sites that were known to produce "fake news" stories and URLs that were ascertained to spread misinformation.[47] The researchers then used a database to track user interactions on social media platforms, focusing on Facebook and Twitter users' interactions with the list of "fake news" sites and URLs. The database counted the shares of, comments on, and likes of the identified sites and URLs on Facebook. On Twitter, it tracked the number of shares. Among other findings, the authors identified that circulation of "fake news" had declined since the time of the 2016 presidential election.

Online activity provides a unique window into users' relationships with media and information on the internet. Such data as shares on social media platforms offer a compelling picture of ML-related behaviors—not participants' perspectives, not multiple-choice responses, but evidence of how they actually interact within the information ecosystem. Rather than addressing specific process-oriented ML competencies, actual online behaviors can be operationalized as outcomes. Because observing activity in this manner can be less evident to participants than in-person observations—or in the case of the second example we offered, not evident to participants at all—Hawthorne effects might be less of a risk. The scale of data that

---

[45] Guess, Nagler, and Tucker, 2019.

[46] Hunt Allcott, Matthew Gentzkow, and Chuan Yu, "Trends in the Diffusion of Misinformation on Social Media," Washington, D.C.: National Bureau of Economic Research, working paper, 2019.

[47] For more details about establishing these lists, see Allcott, Gentzkow, and Yu, 2019.

can be collected in this manner provides more-generalizable findings than the individual measures we have discussed, and all at relatively low cost. The broad trends identified by this research have implications for our society at large.

Of course, there are limitations to using broad data sets of online activity to assess ML competencies. First, although the larger trends identified are valuable, these data are not meant to address specific competencies. They could reveal some of the end results of ML-related proficiency, but not necessarily the processes that led to that result. For example, identifying the number of times a "fake news" article was shared does not offer us specific data about whether individuals are assessing credibility, and how. Although valuable and relevant to our pursuit of understanding how ML competencies are measured, work with these data is conducted at a different scale today than what we seek from studies investigating ML intervention outcomes. Accordingly, we did not find examples of how large-scale online activity data could be applied to measure change in ML competencies within targeted groups of individuals who had participated in an intervention. Given the creativity and technological savvy of members of the ML research community, however, we can imagine this form of data collection being utilized for this purpose in the future.

We have other concerns about using online data to study ML competencies. Given challenges related to privacy and data collection, there need to be extensive safeguards in place to ensure the protection of participant privacy, and individuals might be understandably reticent to have their activities observed. Additionally, tracking online interactions does not capture a wider variety of media forms that are still relevant in today's society despite the dominance of the internet. Other measures leave open the possibility for measuring ML competencies as applied to television news or print media.

Across Measures of ML Competency

The varied types of ML measures outlined in this chapter make evident the dispersed nature of measures related to ML. We drew these measures from the fields of ML, news literacy, information literacy, digital literacy, civics education, and economics, among others. It is evident across the example measures that the foci of these studies are interconnected. The variety in ML measurement is useful in that it paints a multifaceted picture of ML in diverse contexts. However, such variation limits our confidence in broad conclusions drawn from ML literature. From these examples, we see how aggregating findings across relevant research can be a challenge.

Summary

The variety of ML measures discussed are representative of those found in ML studies, each with unique strengths and weaknesses. Our discussion highlights the tensions that ML researchers can encounter when designing or selecting measures for study—some of the measures that might better match the complex or process-oriented competencies linked to ML also come saddled with practical constraints. For instance, portfolio measures might be beneficial for understanding participant research processes, but they are time-intensive, could be difficult to scale, and introduce questions of reliability.

Although common measures are not required, and although there can be benefits from surveying a diverse set of different metrics, there are reasons why having at least some common ground could be valuable. Without some agreement on ML competencies or commonality across ML measures, the degree to which evidence can be aggregated is limited. Aggregated evidence is important in identifying patterns of what works and what does not; this evidence helps inform policy, identify challenges, and guide adjustments in the field. Often, funding decisions hinge on aggregated evidence, not individual studies. We do not believe that creating one singular set of ML competencies or one agreed-on measure is feasible or even preferable. There is no need to abandon the varied approaches to ML that have developed in recent decades. There is an opportunity, however, to start a dialogue about the commonalities that exist across competencies and measures in ML-related studies, and potentially to develop a shared approach that would allow the diverse research in this field to accumulate in a more productive manner. If ML studies are able to speak across disciplines, they can build on one another, not only leading to more generalizable conclusions to assist in decisions around ML but also possibly contributing to a greater profile of ML at a time when it appears to be needed. We explore this recommendation further in Chapter Six.

CHAPTER FIVE

An Inventory of Publicly Available News and Information Literacy Resources

In this chapter, we discuss prepackaged curricula, sets of lesson plans, and other resources developed to facilitate ML education in schools, universities, and among adults. These resources focus on news and information literacy, and we feature both stand-alone programs and modular resources that could be integrated into existing courses or everyday life. Each resource is available to the general public, some free and some at a cost, at the time of the publication of this report.

This chapter is intended to provide some insight into the types of ML resources focused explicitly or primarily on news and information. It could be useful to researchers interested in programs for study, educators and parents looking for ML curricula or activities, and those interested in developing related resources themselves. Although each of these many efforts aims at a similar goal—improving the ability of students to become responsible consumers of and participants in the information ecosystem—there is not clear evidence of coordination or cooperation among developers of these various programs.

This chapter is not an endorsement or a review of research related to any specific ML resource. We have not evaluated these resources, and there is no empirical research connected to the vast majority of them. Rather, the database provides a centralized collection of available resources for ML education that interested parties can explore, and this chapter provides descriptive information about the types of resources available as a whole.

As of the writing of this report, interested parties exploring ML resources have limited options for doing so, with a few centralized repositories available.[1] The Alliance of Civilizations ML Clearinghouse offers a curated collection of ML resources; this site focuses primarily on guides and handbooks, with fewer lesson plans or predeveloped resources and curricula.[2] Frank Baker's Media Literacy Clearinghouse offers a more extensive range of curricula, lesson plans, activities, and other types of resources for educators, parents, and adults.[3] It provides limited summary information about the resources featured; users must visit and assess each resource individually, which can be time-consuming. Furthermore, we found that several of the resources are outdated or no longer active, which is likely a common challenge given ongoing changes in the field and the nature of online resources. We did not find a straightforward and publicly available way to locate, review, and compare ML programs or materials where they exist.

Our database—outlined in a separate, online appendix to this report available for download at www.rand.org/t/RR3050—attempts to address these gaps in a few ways. We sought to provide a resource for exploring ML curricula available to interested parties, such as educators, parents, researchers, and other interested individuals. We provide the following information about each resource in the database, where available: format, how the course is taught, its length, its target audience, and the focal skills it aims to teach. This information facilitates comparison across resources and provides an "at a glance" view of each resource. One key observation drawn from the database is that there is a lack of evaluations of mainstream ML curricula—or, at the least,

---

[1] There are also other, smaller websites that host relevant ML information, including some maintained by experts we interviewed. The database we have put together is different in that it provides not only links but also information about each program—format, duration, audience—that can guide those looking for media literacy tools.

[2] See United Nations Alliance of Civilizations, Media and Information Literacy: Resources," webpage, undated.

[3] See Frank Baker, "Concepts: Media Literacy," Media Literacy Clearinghouse webpage, undated.

a lack of publicly available evaluation information.[4] The What Works Clearinghouse, a central and respected database for educational interventions that provides scientific evidence on what works and what does not when it comes to student outcomes, does not feature studies of ML programs.[5] But as noted elsewhere in this report, such research can inform decisionmakers at the individual, organizational, and systems levels when they are deliberating about ML programming.

Because of the number and diversity of materials online and our own resource limitations, we could not comprehensively survey all ML resources in existence. Instead, we highlight the set of resources most directly focused on what might be called news or information literacy. We made this decision for several reasons. First, as noted in the introduction, we come to ML with an interest in understanding how ML education can work to counter the trends of Truth Decay. The set of resources focused on news and information literacy are directly relevant to this question. Second, attention on ML in the face of an evolving media ecosystem has been significantly focused on how ML education—and specifically information or news literacy— might serve as an antidote to the spread of disinformation and misinformation online. However, we wish to emphasize that the field of ML is much broader, and that although information and news literacy are important, they are no more important than any other type of ML or any other context in which ML education is used. On a final note, we used news and information literacy as a frame for this first cut and chose to document publicly available resources specifically in this area, but we hope in future work to expand this database. We provide more information on the contents of the database in the following sections.

---

[4] To ascertain whether a program had been evaluated, we searched relevant academic publications and program websites. We considered an *evaluation* to be any study that formally assessed participant ML competencies before and after completing an ML program. We consider a *rigorous evaluation* to be one that includes at least a pre-/post-test of an ML curriculum and a control population. Studies that use only a pre-/post-test or only a control/treatment sample might provide correlational research but are second-best.

[5] See Institute of Education Sciences, What Works Clearinghouse website, homepage, undated.

In this chapter, we first explain our approach to building this database. Then, we describe key trends in the landscape of ML resources, such as primary formats, target audiences, and skills taught. In our discussion, we provide several different examples of available educational resources and describe their strengths and weaknesses. However, we do not mention every single resource in the database, nor do we provide a comprehensive description of each. Detailed information about each curriculum, set of lessons, or other ML resource can be found in the database, outlined in the online appendix.

Approach

Inclusion Criteria

Our database consists of ML curricula, lesson plans, activities, webinars, videos, and games. We included resources aimed at a variety of topics—from ML skills to the history of media—and all audiences. As noted, we focused our search on curricula that dealt primarily with information and news literacy, not with ML writ large. Practically, this meant that we excluded programs focused only or primarily on advertising, on entertainment (e.g., video games), and on ML as it pertained primarily to health (e.g., body image or smoking). We also excluded programs focused only or primarily on civic education or civic literacy, which we view as an important area to explore in the future.[6] This did not mean that programs that touched on advertising or civics were left out—merely that we excluded programs that primarily focused on these topics. Finally, we excluded programs that focused exclusively on data privacy or cybersecurity, although many of the ML programs that we included feature an aspect of data security and privacy modules.

These exclusions are a limitation of our database, but one that was required for several reasons. First, ML is an extensive and diverse field, as described throughout this report, and we did not have the resources

[6] Some programs included in our database do feature one module on civics. Although ML and civics education are closely linked, civics education is too broad and important in its own right to be fully captured in this initial report.

in this project to tackle the entire field or to document all ML-related curricula and courses. Second, as noted in Chapter One, our focus in this report is on the relationship between ML and Truth Decay. By focusing the attention on this narrower segment of ML, this chapter is able to dig more deeply into those resources that we did include. Our hope is that as we continue work in this area, we will be able to expand the database to feature a wider array of ML-related topics.

We scoped the review of educational resources in other ways, too. First, we included only U.S.-based programs. We recognize that extensive work on ML is being conducted outside of the United States, but we chose to focus first on documenting curricula, lessons, and other resources developed specifically with the U.S. context in mind. Again, we hope to be able to expand our scope in the future. A second choice we made concerned the formality that a resource needed in order to merit inclusion. We aimed for inclusivity on this point, covering a variety of different formats and levels of depth. We included one-time programs, videos, and modules, but excluded such resources as fact-sheets, short news clips (divorced from other content), and anything that was less of an educational tool and more of a reference. Having references and guides is certainly valuable, but we focused on resources with an instructional component.

Third, we included only nonpartisan and ideologically neutral programs and teaching platforms. This meant excluding programs affiliated with political or religious organizations, though those organizations might play a role in engaging the public in ML education. Our interviews and literature review made clear that ML should be focused on how people approach, question, consume, and create information, not about the answers that are reached or the type of information produced. Ideological neutrality emerged as a best practice of ML, and so we chose to adhere to that in our database as well.

Finally, our database also follows implicit inclusion criteria: We had to be able to find information about the resources online. This means that organic ML programming integrated into existing courses, homegrown courses taught in single classrooms and schools, and other similar approaches will not be captured in this database. We do, however, include courses aimed at teachers (e.g., those intended to train teachers about how to teach ML), and these courses appear to capture some of the strategies and ideas that might be central to some more-integrated or homegrown courses not captured here.

We emphasize again that this program inventory is not a review of ML literature or research and should not be interpreted as such. We include a large number of publicly available media literacy resources in this database, but we did not find formal evaluations of the vast majority of them. Thus, we pursued this inventory as a distinct line of analysis. In this chapter, we discuss curricula, lesson plans, webinars, and other educational resources that are available online, subject to the limitations and exclusions noted previously. We do not advocate the quality of any resource in this database, but we offer descriptions so that readers are more easily able to compare the material.

Identification of Resources

We relied on multiple sources to build our database. We began by performing a series of web-based searches using a variety of targeted terms intended to surface relevant programs and curricula. Our initial search was guided by a diverse set of search terms (and combinations of these terms): media literacy, media education, teaching, curriculum, information literacy, digital literacy, lesson, class, disinformation, misinformation, news literacy, course, and teaching. Our search terms reflect the focus of our database based on the exclusion criteria previously defined. We also searched for ML resources in other ways. For example, we relied on reports and scholarly articles, some of which identified specific resources, and asked interviewees whether they recommended specific programs. Finally, we benefited from aggregation sites that provided lists of diverse ML resources. Although the initial searches were useful, at least one-half of the programs we ultimately identified emerged through these latter two search methods. We do not claim to have exhaustively identified all ML curricula in existence, for the reasons already noted. However, we did capture a significant sample of well-established resources in this area. We intend this database to be a first cut that will be updated as future efforts emerge.

Organization of the Database

Each entry in our database lists an ML curriculum, webinar, set of lesson plans, or other resource to support ML education. The nature of these resources varies significantly. Some provide a prepackaged, formal curriculum or course syllabi with multiple lesson plans. Others feature a set of short online activities and modules that an educator could use in combination or separately, sequenced in almost any order. Some organizations have multiple curricula aimed at different age groups and targeting slightly different skills. Most organizations offer only one program or set of modules, sometimes along with supporting teacher resources, but there are some organizations that provide multiple different types of programs aimed at different audiences. We created a separate entry for each of these resources. This means that some organizations have multiple entries, one for each of the programs or resources that they offer.[7] We did not, however, create multiple entries for cases in which an organization has a single curricular model adapted for multiple different age groups.

Once we collected the set of programs to be featured, we used the database to describe each organization and its programs along a variety of different dimensions. The following list identifies and defines the dimensions along which we examined ML programs. Multiple team members collected and validated the information.[8] The dimensions serve as useful guidelines for understanding similarities and differences across programs. They are organized as follows:

- **Organization:** Identifies the organization responsible for creating and supporting the curriculum, program, or set of modules
- **Resource Title:** The name of the specific curriculum, program, or set of modules

---

[7] We are confident that we have identified the major course offerings by organization, but we might have missed smaller or older programs or those that are less accessible via public searches.

[8] Each program was independently evaluated by at least two coders. Disagreements were resolved through group discussions.

- **Type of Organization:** Identifies the type of organization that developed the program (e.g., university, nonprofit, or news organization)
- **Brief Summary of Available Programming:** Describes the nature and focus of the course, highlights unique features or mission statements
- **Format:** Describes how the resource is structured; for example, as an academic course lasting a semester or year, a workshop (typically a finite set of meetings and often aimed at adults), a supplement to an academic course, or a certificate program
- **Delivery Method:** Describes how the course is provided to participants, whether in person or through an online platform
- **Intended Audience:** Identifies the intended recipient of the program
- **Year Developed:** Identifies the year the program was developed
- **Cost:** Identifies whether the program is free or requires a fee
- **Primary Topic Areas:** Identifies which of 11 core topics are covered by the course. These topic areas were chosen to cover the ranges of different skills and topics within the application of ML (news and information literacy) considered here. Subject areas were verification/fact-checking, navigating/accessing information, creating and sharing media, digital literacy, evaluating source credibility, separating fact and opinion, fairness and balance, teaching ML, evidence and arguments, the media and advertising industry, laws and regulations.

In addition to these categories, we also created other fields to identify such characteristics as whether the curriculum or resource has a syllabus or specific lesson plan online. Initially, we had fields to collect information about relevant program evaluations or assessments of the programs in our database, including not only formal evaluations of program effectiveness but also studies of usage and implementation. With only a few exceptions, we were unable to find such literature in a publicly available format, so we have dropped these fields from the final database.[9] We discuss the one exception and the general lack of program evaluations in more detail in Chapter Three.

Key Trends and Insights

In this section, we discuss some of the key insights that emerged as we compiled our database of programs, such as the types of organizations that appear to be the most active, the most common types of program formats and focal points, and audiences targeted by many programs (as well as those that seem largely neglected). Overall, we list 50 different educational resources for various audiences. Throughout, we provide examples of specific programs. We intend these examples to be illustrative only; we cannot capture detail on all the programs in the chapter. Our database provides the full list and the relevant categorizations. In choosing examples, we have aimed for diversity, meaning we try to mention many different types of programs rather than focusing only on a handful or trying to identify which programs are the "best" on various measures. In the subsequent sections, we first discuss program format and delivery and then conclude with a discussion of the topics covered in the programs in our database.

Program Format and Delivery

Programs in our database vary in their format and delivery, but there are some general trends. First, there is a mix of in-person and online programming. In-person programming typically involves syllabi or lesson plans that teachers or instructors then need to adapt, develop, and deliver to students. Most online programs can be conducted without direct, in-person supervision. About 50 percent of programs fall into the online category. They can be used in a traditional classroom and might benefit from teacher involvement, but they do not necessarily require educator-led instruction. This category includes an Ari-

[9] This does not mean that such evaluations do not exist; program evaluations might be conducted as case reports kept internal to the developer of the course or curriculum. Nevertheless, we cannot capture such information here.

zona State University online course offered through EdX and an online course offered by the City University of New York, "Making Sense of the News," available through CourseRA.[10] Other programs mix in-person and online instruction. The Common Sense Media program, for instance, has online modules that can be supported by teacher-led instruction.[11] Fifteen of our 50 programs are primarily taught in person, meaning that they are delivered via teacher-based instruction. Several are college courses. The UNESCO teaching materials also aim at in-person instruction but provide significant support to teachers in the form of proposed lesson plans.[12]

The format of provided courses also varies, as broken down in Table 5.1. Approximately one-third of the programs in our database provide full academic courses that last a full semester or year and feature a package of lesson plans, activities, topics, and teacher support. Examples are the Create to Learn curriculum created by Dr. Renee Hobbs at the University of Rhode Island,[13] and the Cyber Civics curriculum, which aims to provide students with the technical and cognitive skills to navigate online information.[14] Both of these options provide detailed lesson plans, activities, and course materials for teachers to use when conducting the course. Several colleges and universities offer ML courses intended to last at least one semester—for instance, those taught through the University of Washington (entitled "Calling BS," described in more detail later in this chapter) and Stony Brook University (which offers the option for virtual or in-person education).[15] As

[10] Arizona State University, "Media Lit: Overcoming Information Overload," online course landing page, undated; City University of New York, "Making Sense of the News: News Literacy Lessons for Digital Citizens," online course landing page, undated.

[11] Common Sense Media, Media Literacy, "Turn Students into Fact-Finding Web Detectives," webpage, undated.

[12] See Divina Frau-Meigs, *Media Education: A Kit for Teachers, Students, Parents and Professionals*, Paris: United Nations Educational, Scientific and Cultural Organization, 2006.

[13] Renee Hobbs, Create to Learn website, homepage, undated.

[14] Cyber Civics, "Cyber Civics Curriculum," webpage, undated-a.

[15] Carl Bergstrom and Jevin West, "Calling Bullshit: Data Reasoning in a Digital World," online course landing page, undated-a; Digital Resource Center, Center for News Literacy,

Table 5.1
Resource Formats

Format	Number of Programs
Academic course (semester or full year)	16
Supplement to academic course	27
Workshop/training	6
Certificate program	1

our interviews and literature reviews suggest, extended courses can be time-consuming for teachers and students, but they are also valuable for several reasons. First, they can cover more ML topics. ML covers a wide variety of diverse competencies, and a longer course might be able to cover more of these competencies. Furthermore, extended immersion in ML topics and practice with ML techniques could help improve student retention and learning. This, of course, is a hypothesis that should be tested. Finally, prepackaged courses and curricula might be easier for teachers with limited ML teaching experience to use.

More than one-half of the educational resources in our database are intended as supplements to an academic course. They are typically delivered in a series of modules or as a set of lesson plans that can be integrated with an existing course or curriculum. This programming is flexible in that it can be added to a school's broader curriculum in smaller pieces—for example, as units to supplement a social studies or history course. An example would be the Newseum-produced Media Literacy Booster Pack, which features a series of online activities intended to build ML skills.[16] These supplementary resources vary: Some resources have only a handful of modules; others are more extensive, such as Read Write Think, which provides more than 250 different lesson plans.[17] Other resources, such as those offered by the News Literacy Project, are flexible

"The Course Pack for Spring 2018," webpage, undated.

16 University of Louisville, "Online Learning Modules," webpage, undated; NewseumED, "Media Literacy Booster Pack," webpage, undated.

17 ReadWriteThink, search results for "Media Literacy Lesson Plans," webpage, undated.

in that they can be taught either as a full course or as a series of modules inserted into existing courses. The News Literacy Project programming is broken into 14 different lessons taught through its online Checkology platform.[18] Finally, it is worth noting that in addition to more-traditional educational resources, programs intended to supplement existing courses also come in somewhat nontraditional forms, such as the Crash Course media series, which consists of series of videos covering such topics as "Media and the Mind" and the history of media.[19] These videos are unique in that they can target multiple audiences and can be used either in a classroom setting or outside the classroom.

As already described in this report, resources that can be integrated into existing classroom lessons, such as modules, could have some advantages. First, they provide flexibility. They can be used in a variety of different contexts, and the educator has control over when they are used and how they are integrated into an ongoing course. This flexibility can be valuable, especially for teachers who might already feel overburdened with requirements and need to think more creatively about how to weave in ML content. They could also be used at home by parents or interested individuals. However, some of these supplement-based programs are more limited in what they provide. Some have relatively few modules or are able to cover only a narrow set of topics. These limitations can be overcome by using a variety of modules or working to expand the set of topics covered with other activities over time.

Our database includes only a handful of what we categorize as workshops or training programs. We define workshops and training programs as providing a finite set of lessons (including a single lesson in some cases) with a relatively narrow focus, intended to provide attendees with a new set of skills or competencies by completion. Workshops are typically significantly shorter than a full course and differ from a course supplement in that content is packaged as a coherent set. For the most part, workshops that are in our database are aimed at adults (teachers, journalists, librarians, or the general public). One example is

[18] News Literacy Project, homepage, undated.

[19] CrashCourse, "Media Literacy Preview," Youtube.com, February 20, 2018.

information literacy programming developed by Library Journals LLC aimed at training librarians to impart the importance and value of ML,[20] and the Poynter News University, which provides a series of webinars focused on news and information literacy targeted at developing journalists.[21]

Finally, our database includes a certificate program, made up of multiple graduate courses and taught through the University of Rhode Island Media Education Lab. The program (the Graduate Certificate in Media Literacy) is aimed at educators, librarians, and media professionals and aims to provide enrollees with the skills needed to analyze, interpret, create, and share information, particularly in the digital space.[22] Although the level of commitment required to earn the certificate is more extensive, the depth of training appears comprehensive.

Intended Audiences

Notable attention has been given to ML as a possible solution to problems of disinformation. However, our database makes it clear that the majority of this energy is targeted at K–12 students and, to a lesser extent, college and university students. There are fewer programs targeted at educators, parents, and the general public. Youth are an appropriate focus because young people are at a formative stage in their development, and skills they learn in their early years could be incorporated as part of their mindset as they move on to college and adulthood. The years spent in K–12 and postsecondary education also present a generally captive audience for ML, whether or not the students have an interest in the topic. By contrast, there are few forums that can gather nonstudent adults in a similar manner. The limited ML

---

[20] First Draft, Verification Course, webpage undated-b; Library Journals LLC, "Fighting Fake News," libraryjournal.com, online session landing page, undated.

[21] Poynter News University, homepage, undated.

[22] University of Rhode Island, "Certificate of Graduate Study in Digital Literacy," webpage, undated.

resources available for adults also belie the fact that adults struggle with the demands of the new information system as well.[23]

Resources that do target adults come in a few primary forms. First, there are programs intended for educators. Although these might help teachers improve their own ML skills, they are largely focused on improving teachers' ability to provide ML education to students. These are often offered alongside student courses. For example, the News Literacy Project offers training for teachers, as does the Newseum. There are also some programs aimed uniquely at teachers. Ohio State University, for instance, offers a workshop for teachers interested in learning more about how to teach ML.[24] The University of Rhode Island graduate certificate, as previously mentioned, is available for educators. Finally, there is the handbook created by UNESCO, which provides guidance on constructing ML lesson plans, curricula, and activities for students. The handbook provides a useful level of detail—while providing significant guidance, it also leaves room for teachers to craft courses and activities appropriate to their classrooms and cultural and political context.[25]

Second, there are a small number of resources aimed at journalists. One example is an online training developed by First Draft—a project from the Harvard Kennedy School—that teaches developing journalists how to do a better job of fact-checking their information, including sourcing and verifying the accuracy of photos. A modified version is offered to the general public.[26] Third, there are resources with modules aimed at parents, such as Common Sense Media and

[23] There are more ML resources aimed at adults in the context of health, media, or financial issues. We do not include these because of the scope of the database, but they might fill some of the gaps identified. However, the lack of ML programs focused more directly on news and information literacy is notable.

[24] Ohio State University, "Fake News Workshop," online course landing page, January 5, 2018.

[25] See Frau-Meigs, 2006.

[26] First Draft, "Education," webpage, undated-a.

Cyber Civics, both of which provide modules for parents seeking to support the ML development of their children.[27]

Finally, there are resources available for the general public. Among these are free online videos and other activities that anyone can download, view, or use to improve ML skills. The Crash Course Media series of videos is one example of such a resource. Another is the Mind Edge program on critical thinking, which covers a variety of ML topics and offers interactive exercises and quizzes to engage the audience.[28] Others appear to be largely intended for school audiences but are accessible to the general public and are marketed in a broad way that could appeal to various age groups. An example would be the ML course provided by Stony Brook University's Center for News Literacy.[29] This course is one of the more extensive and better-known, covering such topics as media bias and credibility, news as a business, verification, misinformation and disinformation, deconstructing media, and information-creation and information-sharing. With course materials online, the course is widely accessible, but the course can also be taken for credit, in person.

ML Course Developers

Organizations active in developing ML curricula that fall within the scope of our review are varied and encompass nonprofits, universities, news companies, and private for-profit organizations. We recognize that this set of organizations might be somewhat dependent on our resource selection criteria.

The most active types of organizations in this area are universities and other academic institutions with media labs or centers for journalism that produce ML programming and curriculum. Within the university domain, the labs serve many purposes, drawing not only from scholars focused on journalism or media studies but also education

---

[27] Common Sense Media, undated; CyberCivics, "For Parents," webpage, undated-b.

[28] MindEdge, "Dig Deeper: Critical Thinking in the Digital Age," online course landing page, undated.

[29] Center for News Literacy, "The Course Pack for Fall 2018," online course landing page, undated.

practitioners and others to help improve the quality of ML programming. Two examples are the Media Education Lab at the University of Rhode Island and the News Co/Lab at Arizona State University.[30] These types of centers serve as focal points of progress and activity in the ML field. Another advantage of these centers is that their curricula and resources are often free to the public or to educators. We have mentioned the value that interdisciplinary work would bring to ML research. Media labs are often interdisciplinary in nature, and courses offered through these labs or as part of such labs might be particularly valuable in filling this gap.

In another example, the University of Washington is known for its "Calling BS: Data Reasoning in a Digital World" course, which covers how to locate false and misleading information, the ways in which statistics and visualization can contribute to the spread of false information, and how individuals can counter false and misleading information.[31] Other universities have similarly developed courses aimed at helping students to navigate the digital media ecosystem and to become better, more informed users and producers of information. These courses vary in the extent to which they are publicly available. Some course materials and syllabi are provided online; others are not. In the latter case, access to the course might require official enrollment in the college or university.

Private education companies also produce resources, often prepackaged curricula, to support ML across age groups. These encompass both online and in-person courses that might be attractive to some audiences because they are often all-inclusive, and they provide training or other support to both teachers and students. In some cases, their cost might put them out of reach to teachers or school districts. These programs tend to be stand-alone courses rather than material to be integrated into preexisting courses. One example would be programs offered by Cyber Civics, which provides a library of modules focused on news and ML and on digital citizenship. The program has a sub-

---

[30] Media Education Lab, homepage, undated-a; Arizona State University News Co/Lab, homepage, undated.

[31] Carl Bergstrom and Jevin West, "Syllabus," webpage, undated-b.

scription cost that covers downloadable lesson plans, teacher support materials, professional development for teachers, and newsletters.[32]

Nonprofits and civil society organizations have long played a role in developing ML programming. Established organizations, such as the News Literacy Project and the Newseum, are active in creating ML programming for children.[33] Many of their courses focus explicitly on news media, but digital media and civics are intertwined, and some have a wider remit, covering the creation of media and the role of advertising. Some of these courses come with a cost; others are free.

News companies are also active in the creation of ML curricula and educational resources, and on news literacy in particular. Examples are curricula developed by PBS. These resources often have a very particular orientation toward news information and helping individuals become more discerning consumers, sharers, and creators of news information in particular. For example, the PBS News Hour Student Reporting Labs program provides a series of lessons aimed at teaching students how to be reporters, such as how to choose story topics, research a story, construct arguments, and produce media of all types.[34] Finally, it is worth noting that Google, although not exactly a news company, is also active in this area. Google is the primary sponsor of the "Be Internet Awesome" video, curriculum, and other educational materials focused on digital literacy, and which we added to our database.[35] These materials incorporate games with educational lesson plans and activities that could be used by parents or teachers to spread ML.

It is worth noting that because our selection criteria excluded generalized resources, our assessment of active players in this space does not fully develop the role played by other relevant stakeholders. First, several of the large tech platforms are increasingly active in the ML space, either with advertising campaigns focused on educating the gen-

---

[32] Cyber Civics, "Frequently Asked Questions," webpage, undated-c.

[33] For example, see PBS Kids, "Getting the Most from the Internet," video, "Ruff Ruffman: Humble Media Genius," webpage, undated; Newseum, "Media Literacy," webpage, undated.

[34] PBS News Hour, Student Reporting Labs, "Lesson Plans," webpage, undated.

[35] Google, "Be Internet Awesome," webpage, undated.

eral public about how to spot false information or how to broaden the diversity of their media diet or by funding the development of ML courses and resources. As an example, one of the first funders of Arizona State University's News Co/Lab's ML efforts was Facebook.[36] In addition, our database does not capture the full set of activities by news organizations. The *New York Times*, for example, has developed a series of study guides to accompany its articles, and it also produces a "Kids Edition" once a month to help engage students in news information.[37]

Cost

Because we are also interested in accessibility of ML programs, we considered cost information. More than one-half of the programs in our database are free, open to any individual who wishes to explore the curriculum or use the resources (see Table 5.2). Some examples of free programs are the Crash Course videos, the Newseum activities, curriculum offered through the University of Texas at Austin, and the American Press Institute courses. Another 40 percent of programs have a fee of some kind. This fee could be the cost of buying a prepackaged curriculum or subscribing to a digital one, such as the News Literacy Project. Fees could also be tuition that is paid to enroll in a university providing a relevant course, or costs associated with single courses, in cases where that is an option. Finally, there are courses in our database that are free to audit and have a cost if the student wishes to receive

Table 5.2
Resource Cost

Format	Number of Programs
Free	28
Fee or Tuition	20
Free to audit/cost for credit/certificate	3

[36] "Facebook Support Launches News Co/Lab at ASU to Improve Public Understanding of News, with McClatchy as Its First Newsroom Partner," Walter Cronkite School of Journalism and Mass Communication, Arizona State University, press release, October 3, 2017.

[37] "Lesson Plans," Learning Network landing page, *New York Times*, undated.

course credit or receive a completion certificate at the end, such as the EdX course offered through Arizona State and the Stony Brook News Literacy curriculum.

This review suggests that even for parents, educators, and interested individuals with limited resources, a variety of different ML resources are likely to be available to those who have access to the internet. One possible area for future study could be an analysis of the extent to which the cost of available resources affects access to ML education in a way that might disadvantage certain constituencies.

Core Program Focal Points

With these basic details in mind, we now turn to a review of the substantive content of the courses and curricula that we identified. We emphasize the caveat, which we will discuss in more detail, that our assessment and the coverage of different topic areas is shaped by our sample frame—that is, the types of resources that we targeted for inclusion and exclusion.

We explored the substantive content of the ML resources in our database using an 11-category framework. The 11 focal areas used in our framework cover core ML competencies—with an emphasis on the news and information literacy frame applied in this chapter—that emerged from our review of literature and interviews. These categories are not mutually exclusive. We sought to identify which of the resources in our database covered which focal areas and then analyzed frequencies and patterns. Table 5.3 lists each of the 11 focal areas and notes how many resources covered each topic. At the top of the list is evaluating source credibility—which makes sense, given that questioning and analyzing media and media messages is at the core of ML, whether we are talking about news literacy or ML more broadly. This is followed by verification and fact-checking and creating and sharing media. Verification and fact-checking has been a major area of focus recently because it is seen as one way to combat the spread of disinformation and misinformation that easily proliferates online. It is also a core focus for news and information literacy, the emphasis of most resources in our database. Competencies related to creating and sharing media also have been at the forefront of ML conversations, as the

Table 5.3
ML Course Focal Areas

Focal Area	Number of Programs
Evaluating source credibility	40
Verification/fact-checking	31
Creating/sharing media	29
Navigating/accessing information	26
Separating fact and opinion	26
Fairness and balance	23
Digital literacy	22
Media and adverting industry	22
Evidence and argument	22
Teaching ML	19
Laws and regulations	15

democratized media ecosystem makes it increasingly easy for anyone to become an information and media producer.

Other competencies that rank highly are navigating and accessing information, an increasingly important skill in a crowded media environment; separating factual information from opinion; and being able to identify media bias, fairness, and balance. Our analysis shows that only about one-half of the resources in our database cover "digital literacy" in an explicit way—that could mean a module focused explicitly on social media or internet searches or on the roles of algorithms and aggregators. However, it is important to note that the focal areas listed in Table 5.3 apply equally to conventional and online media, so even resources that do not explicitly focus on digital media might provide students with skills relevant to online media use.

Near the bottom of our list are laws and regulation, teaching ML, evidence and argument, and media and advertising. The fact that fewer of our programs focus on these focal areas is, in part, a function of our sampling frame. We focused on resources oriented toward news and information literacy and intentionally excluded programs that had advertising, health, or violence (among other topics) as their primary focus. That so many of the courses we captured touch on advertising anyway reflects the importance of advertising as a driver of news content and presentation—and also as a key source of bias. We did not look for ML courses that touch on the legal aspect of the media system. Where this came up, it was typically in the context of the First Amendment or intellectual property.

That more of our programs did not focus on the teaching of ML is likely driven by our search strategy but could also reflect that resources to support and train educators to teach ML continue to be somewhat limited. Certainly, such resources as the UNESCO teacher's handbook and support materials offered by such organizations as Common Sense Media, Cyber Civics, and the News Literacy Project have begun to fill this gap. However, there seems to be a need for more publicly accessible teacher-oriented resources, at least in the field of news and information literacy on which we are focused. This gap was one pointed to by some of our interviewees, as well.

We also consider which of our 50 resources cover the largest number of the 11 focal areas identified in our analysis. Looking at aggregate statistics, the mean of all 50 programs is at 5.5, with a low value of 3 and high value of 11. Table 5.4 shows the full distribution, with about one-half of programs covering between five and seven of the 11 categories. Several programs cover all 11 areas, such as the News Literacy Project, the Center for Media Literacy's "Media Lit Kit," the Graduate Certificate program offered by the University of Rhode Island, and American Press Institute's news literacy curriculum.[38] Several capture ten of the defined topic areas, including the Cyber Civics program. Project Look Sharp, the NewseumEd lesson plans and activities, the Poynter News University Webinars, and the Create to Learn curriculum all also cover at least seven of the 11 topics.

No resource covers fewer than three of the 11 categories. Covering few of the 11 topic areas should not be viewed as a negative or as indicative of a less-effective ML resource. It is simply an indication that either the resource has a more narrow focus (and in some cases digs

---

[38] American Press Institute, *Introductory News Literacy*, Arlington, Va., 2013.

Table 5.4
Resources by Number of Categories Covered

Number of Focal Areas	Number of Resources
11	3
10	3
9	0
8	2
7	4
6	6
5	14
4	8
3	10
2	0
1	0

deeper on those areas that it does cover) or that its focus only partly overlaps with the set of 11 areas we used to assess these resources. For example, the First Draft Verification training covers only three categories, but it does so at considerable depth and is intended largely as a tool for journalists and the general public to verify information online.[39]

Teacher Training Programs

We have alluded to teacher training at several points. Our database captures teacher training resources in two ways. First, we have teacher training that is offered as part of a curriculum. These trainings typically focus on providing educators with the skills and tools that they need to implement the curriculum in question and to effectively communicate key messages to students. The News Literacy Project, for

[39] This analysis is based on coding completed independently by two researchers. Differences were adjudicated through discussion. Coding is based on our best assessment of materials publicly accessible online. Programs differed in the depth and completeness of materials provided. Please contact the authors with disagreement or proposed correction to the coding.

instance, offers extensive resources for teachers, providing both online programming and the option of hiring instructors to provide in-person support.[40] Second, the database includes teacher training programs offered as independent workshops and programs geared toward teachers. About one-third of the resources in our database that cover teaching ML take the form of stand-alone workshops or, as in the case of the University of Rhode Island Media Education Lab, full courses. These programs aim to increase the efficacy of ML education not only by teaching best practices but also by providing educators with some of the theory behind ML, why it is important, and contexts that favor student learning.[41] Seminars offered by Ohio State University and through Library Journals LLC are two examples of stand-alone training oriented toward teachers. The rest of the teacher-oriented resources in our database are offered in the form of support materials that accompany courses geared toward students. One example of such support materials is the resources offered by UNESCO; the University of Rhode Island offers guides for teachers and a graduate certificate in ML for teachers, librarians, and college faculty.[42]

Year Developed

About 75 percent of the programs in our database were developed in 2015 or after. This could be a function of our sampling frame—news and information literacy have gained increasing currency as the media ecosystem has evolved, so our focus on this application of ML likely skews our sample toward programs that were developed more recently. This also is likely a result of the nature of online resources that are

---

[40] News Literacy Project, undated.

[41] Renee Hobbs, codirector of the Media Education Lab at the University of Rhode Island, has also developed and validated a 48-item scale aimed at assessing teacher motivations for digital and media literacy. This scale could support teacher training. See Renee Hobbs, *Extending the Digital Literacy Competencies of Teachers*, Chicago, Ill: paper presented to the American Educational Research Association, April 18, 2015; and Renee Hobbs and Sait Tuzel, "Teacher Motivations for Digital and Media Literacy: An Examination of Turkish Educators," *British Journal of Educational Technology*, Vol. 48, No. 1, January 2017.

[42] Media Education Lab, "Graduate Certificate in Digital Literacy," webpage, University of Rhode Island, undated-b.

regularly updated, swapped out, or removed from the internet altogether—meaning that they might not remain available for long as a function of the medium.

Summary

Through a description of the ML resource database provided as an online appendix, we summarized the state of courses, curricula, and other educational resources available in news and information literacy. We highlighted the diversity of currently available programs in terms of format, delivery method, and audience. While some programs provide a full-service curriculum, others were made up of modules, lesson plans, videos, and activities of varying length. Thus, teachers who wish to pursue ML programming have various choices, many freely accessible, for how to do so. Existing resources in the news and information literacy area tend to focus on K–12 students, especially middle and high schoolers, and on college and university students to a lesser extent. There are some programs for educators, and a smaller number created for journalists or with resources aimed at parents. There are also courses available to the general public—these are not always widely publicized and can require user initiative.

The variety of available ML resources provides several options that can be mixed and matched to better fit specific learning objectives. There is a good deal of overlap across the different programs, with many similar courses and activities produced by different groups and aimed at similar audiences. We wonder whether this redundancy could be better funneled using interorganizational efforts. More importantly, there is limited publicly available empirical evidence to support the choice of one course or set of lessons over another, which might create challenges for those unsure of which resource is most appropriate for their needs. As noted elsewhere, this empirical data might very well exist, collected by the developer of the resource and circulated internally; it is not widely published in academic journals or stand-alone reports in the public domain. More publicly available assessment information would be valuable, both for informing educator decisions about which resources to employ in their own classrooms and for contributing to the refinement of existing media literacy courses and curricula.

It is worth noting that the gap between practice and publicly available evaluation data is one that is not uncommon in educational research, beyond ML. Educational research is not lacking efforts to collect student performance data, but a similar search for evaluations of publicly available resources in other content areas might return similarly sparse results.[43] In the case of ML, this gap appears to be exacerbated by a lack of consensus about how to define and measure ML competencies. Committing resources to this endeavor should be a point of focus for those working in this field. In the next chapter, we discuss other high-priority areas that emerge from a synthesis of the research documented here.

---

[43] Matthew Militello, Lisa Bass, Karen T. Jackson, and Yuling Wang, "How Data Are Used and Misused in Schools: Perceptions from Teachers and Principals," *Education Sciences*, Vol. 3, No. 2, 2013; Neil Selwyn, "Data Entry: Towards the Critical Study of Digital Data and Education," *Learning, Media and Technology*, Vol. 40, No. 1, 2015; Monica Bulger, *Personalized Learning: The Conversations We're Not Having*, New York: Data and Society Research Institute, working paper, July 22, 2016.

CHAPTER SIX

A Way Ahead for Media Literacy Education

Truth Decay threatens important facets of U.S. society, at the center of which is the informed, civil discourse that undergirds our democracy. Our review suggests that ML does hold promise as a counterweight to the trends comprising Truth Decay, but that in order to leverage the insights of ML for this purpose, we must build on and make use of the diverse body of knowledge developed in the ML field. In this report, we have identified insights from experts and existing research that can facilitate an application of ML to the challenges that Truth Decay presents, but we have also identified important limitations to leveraging ML in this way. In this chapter, we offer a set of general takeaways, as well as several that are specific to Truth Decay. Then, we provide recommendations aimed at advancing the study of ML, both writ large and with an eye toward the specific challenges motivating this inquiry.

Key Takeaways

Although ML Is Typically Defined by a Core Set of Competencies, There Remain Disagreements Around the Application and Prioritization of Those Competencies

There appears to be general consensus around a broad definition of ML as the ability to access, analyze, evaluate, and communicate media messages—or some close variation on these competencies.[1] Yet our interviews, review of literature, and inventory of programs underscored

[1] Aufderheide, 1993.

that the ML field is diverse, with many specialized subfields and some disagreements about how ML should be explicitly defined. In studies relevant to ML, researchers selected particular framings as associated with their topics of interest. These varied widely but coalesced around themes related to economic motivations, civic engagement and democratic participation, and evaluations of information quality. Some of the variation in how ML was conceptualized in the literature might be related to the diverse set of disciplines that contribute to this field. Precisely how ML is defined in studies matters because it is linked to the outcomes measured, and therefore has a tangible influence on research. We currently find that a wide variation of outcomes are measured in ML, a situation that provides a multifaceted picture of the field but presents a challenge to aggregating evidence.

Although defining ML in specific ways matters for research, experts we interviewed underscored that ML is also a worldview, or a holistic approach to interacting with the information ecosystem. ML competencies, in other words, can be applied across an unlimited number of contexts. For instance, teaching the ability to evaluate sufficiency of evidence for a claim does not have to be relegated to discrete ML courses—this is a competency that can be applied in all academic areas, from science to history. It is also valuable in real-life interactions with the information ecosystem, which is where this competency relates to our pursuit of limiting Truth Decay. If individuals are skilled in their ability to evaluate the sufficiency of evidence for a claim, they will be less likely to trust in, create, or share biased, misleading, and false information. For ML to build resiliency to false information in the news media, in politics, and elsewhere, it will not be enough to teach students skills that apply to specific areas. Instead, a more significant shift in the way we interact with all information is required.

Importantly, the more participatory and active competencies of ML, such as creating and sharing media, could require particular attention in our current environment. Because technology increasingly allows us to generate and disseminate information, the emphasis of ML cannot be exclusively on media consumption. There is some evidence that using creation as an approach to teaching ML competencies is effective.[2] This focus on participatory competencies aligns with the frame of Truth Decay that we bring to the report; our interest is in understanding how ML education can support individuals' resilience to misleading and false information, including their ability to understand information sources and construction, to evaluate quality and credibility, and to create, share, and engage with information in a manner reflective of its quality.

Context Is Key—Both in Designing ML Programs and Applying ML Competencies

One finding to emerge from our interviews is that ML competencies are naturally dependent on individuals' perspectives. This implies particular considerations for creating curricula and resources and for teaching ML.

For an ML resource to be applicable in various contexts, it should be designed to be transferrable. One way we learned this might be achieved in the K–12 educational setting would be to integrate ML across the school day. Teachers could learn how to apply ML in different settings, considering it a method for approaching instruction. Such competencies as identifying credibility of sources, evaluating the sufficiency of evidence for claims, and sharing information in a responsible manner are relevant in all core classes and could be adjusted for different age groups. This would make ML applicable in varied contexts, which could be difficult for more-prescriptive curricula. It is not clear that all schools have the resources to train teachers in this approach or what the analogue would be for adult ML education. It is also unclear whether this is a demonstrably more effective approach than teaching ML through explicit, stand-alone courses; we see this as a crucial area for future research.

Considering context also means that ML curricula should be sensitive to the particular background experiences of the audience. A relevant example from the perspective of Truth Decay relates to the importance of political context. As an interviewee discussed with us, even ML that is provided in a nonpartisan and objective manner might be interpreted dif-

---

2 Banerjee and Greene, 2006.

ferently by audiences, depending on their political perspectives. According to this interviewee, those designing and delivering ML should carefully consider the examples and activities they provide. It is important to focus on teaching participants *how* to think without dictating *what* to think. ML should not provide an answer, for example, as to whether an individual should agree with a political advertisement; it should instead teach individuals to be thoughtful about the purpose and construction of that advertisement, the defensibility of the arguments it makes, and whether and how they want to share that advertisement further. Some experts who study ML in civic and democratic engagement also might argue that ML should teach individuals how to make further decisions based on that information; for instance, how to critique an advertisement publicly or engage politically based on its information.

Wide Variation in ML Outcomes and Measures Presents Challenges to the Field

One specific challenge to aggregating findings across ML studies is the diversity of approaches to defining and measuring ML outcomes employed across the literature. The different types of interventions studied provide a multidimensional picture of ways that ML could develop participant competencies. But because of the dramatically different ways that studies define and measure ML outcomes, it is also difficult to aggregate findings and come away with overarching conclusions. In addition, evidence from ML studies ranges widely from rigorous causal evidence to observational data that is informative but lacks the same empirical weight.

There are several factors that might be contributing to the different ways that ML experts define ML outcomes and design and implement measures of those outcomes. One reason for this variation might be the range of specialization that extends across the ML field, with researchers from different backgrounds bringing divergent—but overlapping—interests related to ML, along with their own methodological traditions. Because of these differences, studies that are conceptually related can end up assessing things that are fundamentally distinct. Another possible contributing factor is the complexity that is built in to ML-related competencies and makes them a challenge to measure in meaningful but practical ways. One topic we introduced in Chapter Four was the tension between complex measures that could assess nuanced ML competencies, such as observational measures, and the limitations of those measures in terms of the investments in cost and time they require. Such investments make these measures difficult to scale.

Several challenges emerge from a lack of agreement in this area. When outcomes do not overlap, for example, it is a challenge to see how studies directly relate to one another. For us to recommend a specific policy-driven move toward furthering the spread of ML educational efforts, it would call for aggregated evidence. A second and related challenge is that we might not yet have a good picture of what the actual effect of ML education is. We might under- or overestimate the effect of ML on participant outcomes because of the difficulties in measuring it.

The development of some common competencies and measures would not only advance research evaluating ML but also facilitate the inclusion of ML in educational testing or national surveying that could provide large data sets for research and could raise ML's profile outside the immediate field. For these reasons, we aver that greater common ground among researchers interested in ML would benefit the field, as we discuss in our recommendations.

Media Literacy Moving Forward

We organize the recommendations in this report by their intended audiences, focusing first on researchers and then on policymakers, practitioners, and the public.

Recommendations for Researchers

Strengthen Interdisciplinary Communication and Collaboration

Our overarching recommendation to researchers in ML is to increase interdisciplinary communication and collaboration at all levels—from data collection to measurement to analysis to application. ML is relevant in journalism, education, communications programs, library sciences, cognitive sciences, sociology, public health, and elsewhere. This variety of applications makes the study of ML rich and multifaceted and helps to ensure that diverse perspectives are accounted for. Each discipline brings its own conceptualization of ML, specific definitions of focal ML competencies, and theoretical histories. These were described to us by several interviewees as siloed disciplines—yet ML is inherently interdisciplinary. Fostering greater collaboration among these disciplines could mitigate several identified challenges in the field.

Collaboration between researchers across ML-related disciplines offers several advantages. First, it could advance ML research by facilitating information sharing and joint study efforts among those with overlapping or complementary interests. Bringing together and aligning such different perspectives could provide increased depth to studies of ML, given that researchers from different fields bring with them their own sets of expertise, and could lead to breakthroughs in the way that ML is studied and measured. Centrally, collaboration could facilitate the identification of a set of common competencies, and even the development of some sets of shared measures, as we will discuss further. Often, researchers from different ML-related literacies overlap conceptually but miss the opportunity to build on relevant work because either they framed ML in a different light or defined the relevant ML competencies in divergent ways.

Second, increased interdisciplinary communication and collaboration offers an opportunity to continue raising awareness of ML outside the research community. With the variety of expertise across ML-related disciplines working for a common purpose, the level of recognition that ML could garner—particularly in a time when policymakers, educators, and the public are seeking solutions to Truth Decay–related problems—could be beneficial to the field and to society. Based on our understanding of the current landscape, we anticipate that recommendations made by a joint commission of ML experts would be valuable to several different audiences, including key decisionmakers in government and education. A unified field of ML-related research also could be important in garnering increased funding. Although a growing number of foundations in the United

States appear invested in ML-related research, ML remains a relatively niche interest. By joining knowledge with influence, it might be possible to attract additional sources of funding for this important field of study.

Mechanisms to Promote Interdisciplinary Collaboration and Communication

There are several possible mechanisms to do this. First, we recommend an interdisciplinary forum that meets regularly to discuss and present work, identify field-wide needs and priorities, and develop cross-disciplinary research that builds on various types of expertise. Interviewees noted some examples in which ML-related stakeholders have gathered for cross-disciplinary convenings in the past, but these do not appear to be ongoing collaborations. Reaffirming a goal of building regular, interdisciplinary communication, with specific goals for outputs and outcomes, could jumpstart greater collaboration. We imagine this effort would need to be organized by leaders from multiple strands of ML. Another approach would be to fund interdepartmental ML fellowships that would allow researchers in one area to work in another. An ML researcher focused on news literacy, for example, could spend time working in digital literacy or critical media literacy. This type of experience could build cross-departmental cooperation. Foundations could also play a role here, as they could fund these types of exchanges, or fund interdisciplinary research proposals, creating incentives for researchers to seek diversity in their professional partnerships. Such efforts as these take time to become institutionalized. Once they are, they would create clear channels of communication and lasting incentives for joint work while strengthening the foundation of ML research for future work in this field.

Areas of Focus for Collaboration

Although there are any number of possible topics on which the interdisciplinary commission could begin its work, we identify two as prime candidates. First, we suggest a focus on creating a set of shared ML competencies and measures that are relevant and applicable across ML subfields. This will require (1) understanding and defining the overlap in the way that ML competencies are defined across subfields and (2) developing a set of measures that adequately capture the complexities of those competencies. To be clear, we do not suggest that all ML subfields drop their unique competencies or decide on using only a single form of measure. Identifying where there are commonalities, however, could ground research across areas of study. A set of well-defined, shared competencies could serve as the basis for research and practice in such areas as news literacy, information literacy, and digital literacy, among others, while each could maintain its own unique competencies in addition to the common set. Throughout this report, we have noted challenges inherent to assessing ML competencies; in Chapter Four, we summarized several existing measures and approaches to assessment used to evaluate ML competencies today. These existing measures present valuable starting points, but as noted, there are significant drawbacks to each. The shortcomings of these measures are not distinct to ML—for instance, the weaknesses of self-reporting are applicable regardless of the subject matter. However, the complexity of ML competencies is unique and makes it more difficult to develop measures that are both adequately nuanced and scalable. The variety of ways that ML competencies are defined and measured presents a challenge to synthesizing research across the literature. As one interviewee noted, evaluating ML competencies and studying progress over time will require a new way of measuring ML skills. This would require conversation and agreement around best practices for capturing such difficult-to-measure competencies, drawing from the varied expertise of those in ML-related fields and from those outside of ML fields who have experience developing innovative measures for complex skills.

This effort is ideally suited to be carried out by an interdisciplinary commission of the type recommended here. The commission's goal would be to identify areas of overlap in ML competencies among fields and then develop and validate a shared set of measures that capture those shared competencies, acknowledging that each group could maintain its own additional measures. The work of the commission need not be the final word, but it could represent a large step forward and then serve as the foundation for future work. This process would strengthen relationships among the varied factions of ML—

and, importantly, it would allow future research from divergent strands of ML to build on each other.

A second potential area of focus for the interdisciplinary commission would be identifying field-wide data needs and establishing the platforms to collect that data consistently over the longer term. The ML field would benefit from acquiring systematic information about the state of ML nationwide. Although pockets of these data exist, a more routinized and formal process for collecting information about ML education exposure; the use of self-reporting and task-based assessments; and the experiences of adults, students, and teachers could go a long way in identifying where further attention is needed. There are already some efforts to mandate ML surveys to gather similar information at the state level.[3] Establishing a platform at the national level for longitudinal data on ML would provide a valuable resource to educators, researchers, and practitioners, but it could also raise awareness about ML more generally. This effort would be most useful if experts from related subfields were engaged in the development of survey questions and the analysis of resulting data.

A first set of surveys could explore how ML is currently taught in schools. This exploration could include questions about the resources allocated to ML, educators' perceptions of their preparation, and additional supports that educators feel they need. To add to these types of efforts, ideally, we could use nationally representative and annual data collected from individuals that would allow researchers to track trends and study patterns and relationships between ML education and other outcomes. This type of systematic data would be useful for several reasons. First, we must identify ML needs in such areas as resources, training, and support. Second, this information could guide future research efforts and ultimately lead to recommendations (largely for policymakers and school administrators) that are aimed at advancing and tailoring support for ML to maximize impact.

---

[3] For example, see State of Washington, Office of the Superintendent of Public Instruction, "Digital Citizenship, Media Literacy, and Internet Safety Survey Results," webpage, May 2018.

Surveys focusing on the status of ML education could be administered through any number of nationally representative panel surveys—including the RAND American Educator Panels,[4] which have the advantage of allowing researchers to track educator responses over time and across geographic regions and school characteristics. One objective would be to administer the same survey multiple times on a regular basis to track how commitment and attention to ML varies across regions and over time. Importantly, this is a step that can be taken in the near term to start gathering more-standardized information about ML education in the United States. We recognize the limitations of surveys, as discussed in Chapter Four, but given the objective of learning more about the state of ML from educators' perspectives, we suggest that these options are fitting.

Surveys also could be used to explore the ML experience of non-educators (e.g., parents and students). A survey, such as RAND's American Life Panel, could provide a platform for such a nationally representative survey.[5] The ideal survey would collect information about individual exposure to and understanding of ML concepts. As noted in this report, self-reporting is not a format for assessing competencies. The advantage of using a panel survey is that we can leverage the other information that we have about panel participants to better understand how ML fits into Americans' lives. Such information could assist in guiding future research.

Surveys like these could be adapted to contain questions relevant across subfields of ML and could also be designed to address issues of special importance to specific research communities, making this a fruitful area for cross-disciplinary cooperation. There are likely many other topics for which cooperation would be productive; we offer these

4 RAND Corporation, "The American Educator Panels," webpage, undated-a. These panels are a nationally representative sample of educators surveyed by RAND to collect the ideas and opinions of educators on key questions of educational policy and practice.

5 The American Life Panel is a nationally representative panel of about 6,000 individuals ages 18 and up. Surveys are administered online. Individuals who do not have access to the internet or a computer are provided necessary technology. For more information, see RAND Corporation, "RAND American Life Panel," webpage, undated-b.

as initial areas of emphasis in hopes that others will be identified as the collaboration between ML-related fields deepens.

Recommendations for Policymakers, Practitioners, and the Public

Consider the Full Range of ML Competencies

One clear observation that emerged from our analysis is that the ML field pulls from a nuanced body of knowledge, one that was established well before recent increases in attention to the issues of misinformation and disinformation. As a result, we recommend that practitioners and policymakers turning to ML as a response to these challenges consider not only the narrow areas of ML that appear immediately relevant (e.g., fact-checking, searching online) but rather the full body of evidence that exists about the relationship between individuals and the information ecosystem. Increasing the lines of communication between practitioners and researchers can contribute to this work. This would ensure that the nuance associated with past ML research is not lost or diluted as attention shifts from the theoretical to the applied. There are already models for such communication. For example, the Bridging the Gap Project is working to strengthen relationships and communication between international relations researchers and policymakers.[6] It aims at just this sort of effort—the translation of research findings in all their detail and richness to a policy context. The ML field would benefit from utilizing existing models of research-practice partnerships.

As an example of what a more nuanced approach to developing applications of ML might look like, consider one clear observation that emerges from our analysis: context matters. We've seen a tendency among some policymakers to suggest the need for mandatory ML education in schools and, in response, a growth industry of prepackaged curricula and resources similar to those discussed in Chapter Five to meet this need.[7] However, several of our interviewed ML experts suggested that a mandated ML program applied without regard to context is unlikely to get to the root of the problem.

---

[6] Bridging the Gap Project, homepage, undated.

[7] For example, see Ryan J. Foley, "Efforts Grow to Help Students Evaluate What They See Online," Associated Press, December 30, 2017.

Instead, districts, schools, and classrooms should have the flexibility to tailor or develop and apply an approach to ML suited to their particular contexts. Approaches to ensuring that students receive sufficient ML education might be to develop flexible guidelines that allow teachers to select their own ML curricular materials rather than dictating required content, or to provide schools with funding and resources earmarked for training in an approach to ML education of the school's choosing. There are likely any number of other options, and by using ML experts to inform their decisions and policy position, practitioners and policymakers will have a mechanism to explore these options more thoroughly and make better-informed decisions.

Scaling ML Efforts Will Require Participation from Diverse Constituencies

As noted, scaling of ML efforts is both necessary and difficult. The best way to scale ML efforts, it seems, might be to use other agents of ML in addition to teachers, and other forums for ML in addition to schools, such as libraries, churches, community centers, homes, and places of employment. There are already numerous examples of support for ML in faith communities.[8] In these contexts, a pastor or rabbi, a librarian, a parent, or a professional mentor can serve as an agent of ML in both formal and informal ways. Pursuing this type of decentralized approach might be one way to achieve the "herd immunity" that experts we interviewed pointed toward.

For policymakers, the idea that ML education needs to be integrated widely has a few implications. First, both policymakers and practitioners should take steps to empower and support nontraditional agents of ML. This might mean grants for libraries, churches, or other entities interested in providing training courses or implementing other resources in the community. Second, and related to the previous point, policymakers should avoid overly programmatic mandates or policies that might limit the space for these independent efforts or fail to acknowledge the role that these efforts play. This is particularly true

---

[8] For example, see Center for Media Literacy, "Media Literacy in Faith Communities," webpage, undated.

because we have little concrete evidence about what approaches are most effective in different contexts. As of the publication of this report, numerous states have passed ML-related legislation.[9] As this legislation moves through implementation, it will be important to research these efforts—and their effects—to better understand what kinds of legislation manage the balance inherent in mandating work that is integrally context-specific. Third, it might be valuable at the community level to consider maintaining a central portal or site that would provide information on different ML outreach efforts and that could serve as a resource for interested community members.

As a final point, we note that although this recommendation is aimed first at policymakers and practitioners, *it is also a recommendation with important implications for the general public.* If scaling ML relies on the grassroots efforts of individuals across the country, then parents, coaches, bosses, mentors, and friends will play central roles in expanding the reach and effectiveness of ML education. What should be the starting point for someone who wishes to get more involved? For those who are interested, our inventory of resources in Chapter Five might be one point of departure. We have not evaluated these resources for quality or effectiveness—though we hope such research is forthcoming—but descriptive information about each can assist in selection.

---

[9] For example, see Media Literacy Now, Inc., "Media Literacy Legislative Roundup: 21 Bills, 11 States, 5 New Laws," January 2, 2018.

References

Achieve, Inc., *Next Generation Science Standards: For States, by States: Lead States*, Washington, D.C.: National Academies Press, 2013.

Adair, John G., "The Hawthorne Effect: A Reconsideration of the Methodological Artifact," *Journal of Applied Psychology*, Vol. 69, No. 2, 1984, pp. 334–345.

Allcott, Hunt, Matthew Gentzkow, and Chuan Yu, *Trends in the Diffusion of Misinformation on Social Media*, Washington, D.C.: National Bureau of Economic Research, working paper, 2019.

American Association of Colleges and Universities, "ePortfolios," webpage, undated. As of April 25, 2019:
https://www.aacu.org/eportfolios

American Association of School Librarians, *AASL Standards Framework for Learners: National School Library Standards for Learners, School Librarians, and School Libraries*, Chicago, Ill., 2018. As of April 25, 2019:
https://standards.aasl.org/wp-content/uploads/2017/11/AASL-Standards-Framework-for-Learners-pamphlet.pdf

American Library Association's Presidential Committee on Information Literacy, *Presidential Committee on Information Literacy: Final Report*, Washington, D.C., 1989.

American Press Institute, *Introductory News Literacy*, Arlington, Va., 2013. As of April 25, 2019:
https://www.americanpressinstitute.org/wp-content/uploads/2013/10/Introductory-News-Literacy-curriculum.pdf

Arizona State University, "Media Lit: Overcoming Information Overload," online course landing page, undated. As of April 23, 2019:
https://www.edx.org/course/media-lit-overcoming-information-asux-mco425x

Arizona State University News Co/Lab, homepage, undated. As of April 23, 2019:
https://newscollab.org/

Association of College and Research Libraries, *Information Literacy Competency Standards for Higher Education*, Chicago, Ill.: American Library Association, 2000. As of April 25, 2019:
https://alair.ala.org/bitstream/handle/11213/7668/ACRL%20Information%20Literacy%20Competency%20Standards%20for%20Higher%20Education.pdf?sequence=1&isAllowed=y

Aufderheide, Patricia, *Media Literacy: A Report of the National Leadership Conference on Media Literacy*, Washington, D.C.: Aspen Institute, 1993.

Austin, Erica Weintraub, Yi-Chun Chen, Bruce E. Pinkleton, and Jessie Quintero Johnson, "Benefits and Costs of Channel One in a Middle School Setting and the Role of Media-Literacy Training," *Pediatrics*, Vol. 117, No. 3, March 2006, pp. 423–433. As of April 29, 2019:
https://www.ncbi.nlm.nih.gov/pubmed/16510621

Austin, Erica Weintraub, Bruce E. Pinkleton, Yi-Chun Chen, and Bruce W. Austin, "Processing of Sexual Media Messages Improves Due to Media Literacy Effects on Perceived Message Desirability," *Mass Communication and Society*, Vol. 18, No. 4, 2015, pp. 399–421.

Austin, Erica Weintraub, Bruce E. Pinkleton, Stacey J. T. Hust, and Marilyn Cohen, "Evaluation of an American Legacy Foundation/Washington State Department of Health Media Literacy Pilot Study," *Health Communication*, Vol. 18, No. 1, 2005, pp. 75–95.

Baker, Frank, "Concepts: Media Literacy," Media Literacy Clearinghouse webpage, undated. As of April 23, 2019:
http://frankwbaker.com/mlc/media-literacy/

Banerjee, Smita C., and Kathryn Greene, "Analysis Versus Production: Adolescent Cognitive and Attitudinal Responses to Antismoking Interventions," *Journal of Communication*, Vol. 56, No. 4, 2006, pp. 773–794.

Bergsma, Lynda J., and Mary E. Carney, "Effectiveness of Health-Promoting Media Literacy Education: A Systematic Review," *Health Education Research*, Vol. 23, No. 3, 2008, pp. 522–542.

Bergstrom, Carl, and Jevin West, Calling Bullshit: Data Reasoning in a Digital World, online course landing page, undated-a. As of April 23, 2019:
https://callingbullshit.org/index.html

———, "Syllabus," webpage, undated-b. As of April 23, 2019:
https://callingbullshit.org/syllabus.html

Bickham, David S., and Ronald G. Slaby, "Effects of a Media Literacy Program in the US on Children's Critical Evaluation of Unhealthy Media Messages About Violence, Smoking, and Food," *Journal of Children and Media*, Vol. 6, No. 2, 2012, pp. 255–271.

Bridging the Gap, homepage, undated. As of April 25, 2019:
https://bridgingthegapproject.org/

Buckingham, David, Shaku Banaji, Andrew Burn, Diane Carr, Sue Cranmer, and Rebekah Willett, *The Media Literacy of Children and Young People: A Review of the Research Literature on Behalf of Ofcom*, London: Centre for the Study of Children, Youth and Media, 2005.

Bulger, Monica E., "Measuring Media Literacy in a National Context: Challenges of Definition, Method and Implementation," *Media Studies*, Vol. 3, No. 6, 2012, pp. 83–104.

———, *Personalized Learning: The Conversations We're Not Having*, New York: Data and Society Research Institute, working paper, July 22, 2016.

Bulger, Monica, and Patrick Davison, *The Promises, Challenges, and Futures of Media Literacy*, New York: Data and Society Research Institute, February 21, 2018. As of April 23, 2019:
https://datasociety.net/output/
the-promises-challenges-and-futures-of-media-literacy/

California Department of Education, *Model School Library Standards for California Public Schools*, Sacramento, Calif., 2011.

Center for Media Literacy, "Media Literacy in Faith Communities," webpage, undated. As of April 25, 2019:
https://www.medialit.org/reading-room/media-literacy-faith-communities

Center for News Literacy, "The Course Pack for Fall 2018," online course landing page, undated. As of April 23, 2019:
http://drc.centerfornewsliteracy.org/course-pack

City University of New York, "Making Sense of the News: News Literacy Lessons for Digital Citizens," online course landing page, undated. As of April 23, 2019:
https://www.coursera.org/learn/news-literacy

Clarivate Analytics, "Web of Science," webpage, undated. As of April 23, 2019:
https://clarivate.com/products/web-of-science/

Comer, Jonathan S., Jami M. Furr, Rinad S. Beidas, Courtney L. Weiner, and Philip C. Kendall, "Children and Terrorism-Related News: Training Parents in Coping and Media Literacy," *Journal of Consulting and Clinical Psychology*, Vol. 76, No. 4, August 2008, pp. 568–578.

Common Sense Media, "Turn Students into Fact-Finding Web Detectives," webpage, undated. As of April 23, 2019:
https://www.commonsense.org/education/teaching-strategies/
turn-students-into-fact-finding-web-detectives

Conley, David, "A New Era for Educational Assessment," *Education Policy Analysis Archives*, Vol. 23, No. 8, 2015, pp. 1–36.

CrashCourse, "Media Literacy Preview," YouTube.com, February 20, 2018. As of April 23, 2019:
https://www.youtube.com/watch?v=sPwJ0obJya0&list=PL8dPuuaLjXtM6jSpzb5gMNsx9kdmqBfmY&index=1

Crist, Courtney A., Susan E. Duncan, and Laurie M. Bianchi, "Incorporation of Cross-Disciplinary Teaching and a Wiki Research Project to Engage Undergraduate Students to Develop Information Literacy, Critical Thinking, and Communication Skills," *Journal of Food Science Education*, Vol. 16, No. 3, July 2017, pp. 81–91.

Cyber Civics, "Cyber Civics Curriculum," webpage, undated-a. As of April 23, 2019:
http://www.cybercivics.com/curriculum

———,"For Parents," webpage, undated-b. As of April 23, 2019:
http://www.cybercivics.com/for-parents

———, "Frequently Asked Questions," webpage, undated-c. As of April 23, 2019:
http://www.cybercivics.com/frequently-asked-questions

Darling-Hammond, Linda, "Teacher Quality and Student Achievement," *Education Policy Analysis Archives*, Vol. 8, No. 1, 2000, pp. 1–44.

Davenport, David, and Jeffrey Jones, "The Politics of Literacy," *Policy Review*, Vol. 130, No. 2, 2005, pp. 45–57.

Digital Resource Center, Center for News Literacy, "The Course Pack for Spring 2018," webpage, undated. As of May 7, 2019:
https://digitalresource.center/node/17871

Duran, Robert L., Bill Yousman, Kaitlin M. Walsh, and Melanie A. Longshore, "Holistic Media Education: An Assessment of the Effectiveness of a College Course in Media Literacy," *Communication Quarterly*, Vol. 56, No. 1, 2008, pp. 49–68.

Education Resource Information Center, homepage, undated. As of April 23, 2019:
https://eric.ed.gov/

"Facebook Support Launches News Co/Lab at ASU to Improve Public Understanding of News, with McClatchy as Its First Newsroom Partner," Walter Cronkite School of Journalism and Mass Communication, Arizona State University, press release, October 3, 2017. As of April 23, 2019:
https://cronkite.asu.edu/news-and-events/news/facebook-support-launches-news-colab-asu-improve-public-understanding-news

Fan, Xitao, Brent C. Miller, Kyung-Eun Park, Bryan W. Winward, Mathew Christensen, Harold D. Grotevant, and Robert H. Tai, "An Exploratory Study About Inaccuracy and Invalidity in Adolescent Self-Report Surveys," *Field Methods*, Vol. 18, No. 3, 2006, pp. 223–244.

Fingar, Kathryn R., and Tessa Jolls, "Evaluation of a School-Based Violence Prevention Media Literacy Curriculum," *Injury Prevention*, 2013, pp. 183–190.

First Draft, "Education," webpage, undated-a. As of April 23, 2019: https://firstdraftnews.org/en/education/learn/

———, "Verification Course," webpage, undated-b. As of April 23, 2019 (subscription required): https://firstdraftnews.org/en/education/course/verification-curriculum/1/lesson-1-intro-wardle/C4

Fleming, Jennifer, "What Do Facts Have to Do with It? Exploring Instructional Emphasis in the Stony Brook News Literacy Curriculum," *Journal of Media Literacy Education*, Vol. 7, No. 3, 2015, pp. 73–92.

Foley, Ryan J., "Efforts Grow to Help Students Evaluate What They See Online," Associated Press, December 30, 2017. As of April 25, 2019: https://apnews.com/64b5ce49f58940eda86608f3eac79158

Frau-Meigs, Divina, *Media Education: A Kit for Teachers, Students, Parents and Professionals*, Paris: United Nations Educational, Scientific and Cultural Organization, 2006. As of April 24, 2019: https://unesdoc.unesco.org/ark:/48223/pf0000149278

Google, "Be Internet Awesome," webpage, undated. As of February 23, 2019: https://beinternetawesome.withgoogle.com/en_us

Guess, Andrew, Jonathon Nagler, and Joshua Tucker, "Less Than You Think: Prevalence and Predictors of Fake News Dissemination on Facebook," *Science Advances*, Vol. 5, No. 1, 2019, pp. 1–8.

Hallaq, Tom, "Evaluating Online Media Literacy in Higher Education: Validity and Reliability of the Digital Online Media Literacy Assessment (DOMLA)," *Journal of Media Literacy Education*, Vol. 8, No. 1, 2016, pp. 62–84. As of April 25, 2019: http://digitalcommons.uri.edu/jmle/vol8/iss1/5

Hargittai, Eszter, "Survey Measures of Web-Oriented Digital Literacy," *Social Science Computer Review*, Vol. 23, No. 3, Fall 2005, pp. 371–379.

Hargittai, Eszter, Lindsay Fullerton, Ericka Menchen-Trevino, and Kristin Yates Thomas, "Trust Online: Young Adults' Evaluation of Web Content," *International Journal of Communication*, Vol. 4, 2010, pp. 468-494.

Higgins, Joan Wharf, and Deborah Begoray, "Exploring the Borderlands Between Media and Health: Conceptualizing Critical Media Health Literacy," *Journal of Media Literacy Education*, Vol. 4, No. 2, 2012, pp. 136–148.

Hobbs, Renee, Create to Learn website, homepage, undated. As of April 23, 2019: https://createtolearn.online/

———, *Digital and Media Literacy: A Plan of Action. A White Paper on the Digital and Media Literacy Recommendations of the Knight Commission on the Information Needs of Communities in a Democracy*, Washington, D.C.: Aspen Institute, 2010.

———, *Extending the Digital Literacy Competencies of Teachers*, Chicago, Ill: paper presented to the American Educational Research Association, April 18, 2015.

———, "When Teens Create the News: Examining the Impact of PBS News Hour Student Reporting Labs," *Journalism Education*, Vol. 5, No. 1, 2016, pp. 61–73.

Hobbs, Renee, Katie Donnelly, Jonathan Friesem, and Mary Moen, "Learning to Engage: How Positive Attitudes About the News, Media Literacy, and Video Production Contribute to Adolescent Civic Engagement," *Educational Media International*, Vol. 50, No. 4, 2013, pp. 231–246.

Hobbs, Renee, and Richard Frost, "Measuring the Acquisition of Media-Literacy Skills," *Reading Research Quarterly*, Vol. 38, No. 3, 2003, pp. 330–355.

Hobbs, Renee, and Sait Tuzel, "Teacher Motivations for Digital and Media Literacy: An Examination of Turkish Educators," *British Journal of Educational Technology*, Vol. 48, No. 1, January 2017, pp. 7–22.

Institute of Education Sciences, What Works Clearinghouse website, homepage, undated. As of April 23 2019:
https://ies.ed.gov/ncee/wwc/

International Society for Technology Education, "ISTE Standards for Students," webpage, undated. As of April 23, 2019:
http://www.iste.org/standards/for-students#startstandards

Jenkins, Henry, "Confronting the Challenges of Participatory Culture: Media Education for the 21st Century (Part One)," *Nordic Journal of Digital Literacy*, Vol. 2, No. 1, 2007, pp. 23–33.

Jeong, Se-Hoon, Hyunyi Cho, and Yoori Hwang, "Media Literacy Interventions: A Meta-Analytic Review," *Journal of Communication*, Vol. 62, No. 3, 2012, pp. 454–472.

Jolls, Tessa, and Carolyn Wilson, "The Core Concepts: Fundamental to Media Literacy Yesterday, Today and Tomorrow," *Journal of Media Literacy Education*, Vol. 6, No. 2, 2014, pp. 68–78.

Kahne, Joseph, and Benjamin Bowyer, "Educating for Democracy in a Partisan Age: Confronting the Challenges of Motivated Reasoning and Misinformation," *American Educational Research Journal*, Vol. 54, No. 1, 2017, pp. 3–36.

Kahne, Joseph, Nam-Jin Lee, and Jessica Timpany Feezell, "Digital Media Literacy Education and Online Civic and Political Participation," *International Journal of Communication*, Vol. 6, 2012, pp. 1–24.

Katz, Irvin R., "Testing Information Literacy in Digital Environments: ETS's iSkills Assessment," *Information Technology and Libraries*, Vol. 26, No. 3, 2007, pp. 3–12.

Katz, Irvin R., and Norbert Elliot, "Information Literacy in Digital Environments: Construct Mediation, Construct Modeling, and Validation Processes," in Barbara J. D'Angelo, Sandra Jamieson, Barry Maid, and Janice R. Walker, eds., *Information Literacy: Research and Collaboration Across Disciplines*, Fort Collins, Colo.: WAC Clearinghouse and University Press of Colorado, 2016, pp. 93–114.

Kavanagh, Jennifer, William Marcellino, Jonathan S. Blake, Shawn Smith, Steven Davenport, and Mahlet G. Tebeka, *News in a Digital Age: Comparing the Presentation of News Information over Time and Across Media Platforms*, Santa Monica, Calif.: RAND Corporation, RR-2960-RC, 2019. As of June 2019: https://www.rand.org/pubs/research_reports/RR2960.html

Kavanagh, Jennifer, and Michael D. Rich, *Truth Decay: An Initial Exploration of the Diminishing Role of Facts and Analysis in American Public Life*, Santa Monica, Calif.: RAND Corporation, RR-2314-RC, 2018. As of April 23, 2019: https://www.rand.org/pubs/research_reports/RR2314.html

Kellner, Douglas, and Jeff Share, "Toward Critical Media Literacy: Core Concepts, Debates, Organizations, and Policy," *Discourse: Studies in the Cultural Politics of Education*, Vol. 26, No. 3, 2005, pp. 369–386.

Kong, Siu Cheung, "Developing Information Literacy and Critical Thinking Skills Through Domain Knowledge Learning in Digital Classrooms: An Experience of Practicing Flipped Classroom Strategy," *Computers and Education*, Vol. 78, 2014, pp. 160–173.

"Lesson Plans," Learning Network landing page, *New York Times*, undated. As of April 25, 2019:
https://www.nytimes.com/section/learning/lesson-plans

Library Journals LLC, "Fighting Fake News," libraryjournal.com, online session landing page, undated. As of April 23, 2019:
https://learn.libraryjournal.com/courses/fighting-fake-news

Literat, Ioana, "Measuring New Media Literacies: Towards the Development of a Comprehensive Assessment Tool," *Journal of Media Literacy Education*, Vol. 6, No. 1, 2014, pp. 15–27.

Livingstone, Sonia, "Media Literacy and the Challenge of New Information and Communication Technologies," *Communication Review*, Vol. 7, No. 1, 2004, pp. 3–14.

Livingstone, Sonia, and Ellen Helsper, "Gradations in Digital Inclusion: Children, Young People and the Digital Divide," *New Media and Society*, Vol. 9, No. 4, 2007, pp. 671–696.

Livingstone, Sonia, and Nancy Thumim, *Assessing the Media Literacy of UK Adults: A Review of the Academic Literature*, London: Broadcasting Standards Commission, Independent Television Commission, and National Institute of Adult Continuing Education, March 2003.

Maksl, Adam, Stephanie Craft, Seth Ashley, and Dean Miller, "The Usefulness of a News Media Literacy Measure in Evaluating a News Literacy Curriculum," *Journalism and Mass Communication Educator*, Vol. 72, No. 2, 2017, pp. 228–241.

Mandalios, Jane, "RADAR: An Approach for Helping Students Evaluate Internet Sources," *Journal of Information Science*, Vol. 39, No. 4, 2013, pp. 470–478.

Martens, Hans, and Renee Hobbs, "How Media Literacy Supports Civic Engagement in a Digital Age," *Atlantic Journal of Communication*, Vol. 23, No. 2, 2015, pp. 120–137.

McGrew, Sarah, Joel Breakstone, Teresa Ortega, Mark Smith, and Sam Wineburg, "Can Students Evaluate Online Sources? Learning from Assessments of Civic Online Reasoning," *Theory and Research in Social Education*, Vol. 46, No. 2, 2018, pp. 165–193.

Media Education Lab at the University of Rhode Island, homepage, undated-a. As of April 23, 2019:
https://mediaeducationlab.com/

———, "Graduate Certificate in Digital Literacy," webpage, University of Rhode Island, undated-b. As of April 25, 2019:
https://mediaeducationlab.com/graduate-certificate-digital-literacy

———, "Key Ideas from Digital and Media Literacy: Connecting Culture and Classroom," webpage, undated-c. As of April 23, 2019:
https://mediaeducationlab.com/
key-ideas-digital-and-media-literacy-connecting-culture-and-classroom

Media Literacy Now, Inc., "Media Literacy Legislative Roundup: 21 Bills, 11 States, 5 New Laws," January 2, 2018. As of April 25, 2019:
https://medialiteracynow.org/
media-literacy-legislative-roundup-21-bills-11-states-5-new-laws/

Mihailidis, Paul, "Media Literacy in Journalism/Mass Communication Education: Can the United States Learn from Sweden?" *Journalism and Mass Communication Educator*, Vol. 60, No. 4, 2006, pp. 415–428.

Mihailidis, Paul, and Benjamin Thevenin, "Media Literacy as a Core Competency for Engaged Citizenship in Participatory Democracy," *American Behavioral Scientist*, Vol. 57, No. 11, 2013, pp. 1611–1622.

Militello, Matthew, Lisa Bass, Karen T. Jackson, and Yuling Wang, "How Data Are Used and Misused in Schools: Perceptions from Teachers and Principals," *Education Sciences*, Vol. 3, No. 2, 2013, pp. 98–120.

MindEdge, "Dig Deeper: Critical Thinking in the Digital Age," online course landing page, undated. As of April 23, 2019:
https://mindedge.com/page/dig-deeper

National Association for Media Literacy Education, "Media Literacy Defined," webpage, undated. As of April 23, 2019:
https://namle.net/publications/media-literacy-definitions/

National Council of Teachers of English, "NCTE/IRA Standards for the English Language Arts," webpage, undated. As of April 25, 2019:
http://www.ncte.org/standards/ncte-ira

National Governors Association Center for Best Practices, Council of Chief State School Officers, *Common Core State Standards*, Washington, D.C., 2010.

National Research Council, "Indicators," *The Importance of Common Metrics for Advancing Social Science Theory and Research: A Workshop Summary*, Washington, D.C.: National Academies Press, 2011, pp. 31–52.

News Literacy Project, homepage, undated. As of April 23, 2019:
http://www.newslit.org

Newseum, "Media Literacy," webpage, undated. As of April 23, 2019:
http://www.newseum.org/tag/media-literacy

NewseumED, "Media Literacy Booster Pack," webpage, undated. As of April 23, 2019:
https://newseumed.org/collection/media-literacy-booster-pack/

Next Generation Science Standards, "Frequently Asked Questions," webpage, undated. As of April 24, 2019:
https://www.nextgenscience.org/faqs

Ohio State University, "Fake News Workshop," online course landing page, January 5, 2018. As of April 23, 2019:
https://osu.libguides.com/c.php?g=753560&p=5398127

PBS Kids, "Getting the Most from the Internet," video on "Ruff Ruffman: Humble Media Genius," webpage, undated. As of April 23, 2019:
http://pbskids.org/fetch/ruff/

PBS News Hour, Student Reporting Labs, "Lesson Plans," webpage, undated. As of April 23, 2019:
https://studentreportinglabs.org/lesson-plans/

Pinkleton, Bruce E., Erica Weintraub Austin, Yi-Chun Chen, and Marilyn Cohen, "Assessing Effects of a Media Literacy–Based Intervention on US Adolescents' Responses to and Interpretations of Sexual Media Messages," *Journal of Children and Media*, Vol. 7, No. 4, 2013, pp. 463–479.

Porter, Andrew C., "Measuring the Content of Instruction: Uses in Research and Practice," *Educational Researcher*, Vol. 31, No. 7, 2002, pp. 3–14.

Potter, James W., *Theory of Media Literacy: A Cognitive Approach*, Thousand Oaks, Calif.: SAGE, 2014.

Poynter News University, homepage, undated. As of April 23, 2019:
https://www.newsu.org/

Primack, Brian A., Danielle Fine, Christopher K. Yang, Dustin Wickett, and Susan Zickmund, "Adolescents' Impressions of Antismoking Media Literacy Education: Qualitative Results from a Randomized Controlled Trial," *Health Education Research*, Vol. 24, No. 4, 2008, pp. 608–621.

RAND Corporation, "The American Educator Panels," webpage, undated-a. As of April 25, 2019:
https://www.rand.org/education-and-labor/projects/aep.html

———, "RAND American Life Panel," webpage, undated-b. As of April 25, 2019:
https://www.rand.org/research/data/alp.html

Ranieri, Maria, and Francesco Fabbro, "Questioning Discrimination Through Critical Media Literacy: Findings from Seven European Countries," *European Educational Research Journal*, Vol. 15, No. 4, July 1, 2016, pp. 462–479.

Rapchak, Marcia E., Leslie A. Lewis, Julie K. Motyka, and Margaret Balmert, "Information Literacy and Adult Learners: Using Authentic Assessment to Determine Skill Gaps," *Adult Learning*, Vol. 26, No. 4, pp. 135–142.

ReadWriteThink, search results for "Media Literacy Lesson Plans," webpage, undated. As of January 29, 2019:
http://www.readwritethink.org/search/?resource_type=6&type=8&learning_objective=29&sort_order=views

RobbGrieco, Michael, and Renee Hobbs, *A Field Guide to Media Literacy Education in the United States*, Kingston, R.I.: Media Education Lab at the University of Rhode Island, 2013.

Scharf, Davida, Norbert Elliot, Heather A. Huey, Vladimir Briller, and Kamal Joshi, "Direct Assesment of Information Literacy Using Writing Portfolios," *Journal of Academic Librarianship*, Vol. 33, No. 4, 2007, pp. 462–477.

Scull, Tracy M., and Janis B. Kupersmidt, "An Evaluation of a Media Literacy Program Training Workshop for Late Elementary School Teachers," *Journal of Media Literacy Education*, Vol. 2, No. 3, 2011, pp. 199–208.

Scull, Tracy M., Janis B. Kupersmidt, and Tara N. Weatherholt, "The Effectiveness of Online, Family-Based Media Literacy Education for Substance Abuse Prevention in Elementary School Children: Study of the Media Detective Family Program," *Journal of Community Psychology*, Vol. 45, No. 6, 2017, pp. 796–809.

Selwyn, Neil, "Data Entry: Towards the Critical Study of Digital Data and Education," *Learning, Media and Technology*, Vol. 40, No. 1, 2015, pp. 64–82.

Smith, Marshall, and Jennifer O'Day, "Systemic School Reform," in Susan Fuhrman and Betty Malen, eds., *The Politics of Curriculum and Testing: The 1990 Yearbook of the Politics of Education Association*, New York: Falmer Press, 1991, pp. 233–267.

Soland, Jim, Laura Hamilton, and Brian Stecher, *Measuring 21st Century Competencies: Guidance for Educators*, Santa Monica, Calif.: Asia Society and RAND Corporation, 2013. As of April 25, 2019: https://asiasociety.org/files/gcen-measuring21cskills.pdf

Stanford History Education Group, homepage, undated. As of April 25, 2019: https://sheg.stanford.edu

State of Washington, Office of the Superintendent of Public Instruction, "Digital Citizenship, Media Literacy, and Internet Safety Survey Results," webpage, May 2018. As of April 25, 2019: http://www.k12.wa.us/EdTech/DigitalCitMediaLit/default.aspx

Stecher, Brian M., and Laura S. Hamilton, *Measuring Hard-to-Measure Student Competencies: A Research and Development Plan*, Santa Monica, Calif.: RAND Corporation, RR-863-WFHF, 2014. As of April 24, 2019: https://www.rand.org/pubs/research_reports/RR863.html

Tongco, Tricia, "How People Can Combat Fake News," ATTN.com, December 2, 2016. As of April 23, 2019: https://archive.attn.com/stories/13234/how-people-can-combat-fake-news

Tully, Melissa, and Emily K. Vraga, "Effectiveness of a News Media Literacy Advertisement in Partisan Versus Nonpartisan Online Media Contexts," *Journal of Broadcasting and Electronic Media*, Vol. 61, No. 1, 2017, pp. 144–162.

UNESCO—*See* United Nations Educational, Scientific and Cultural Organization.

United Nations Alliance of Civilizations, "Media and Information Literacy: Resources," webpage, undated. As of April 23, 2019: https://milunesco.unaoc.org/mil-resources/

United Nations Educational, Scientific and Cultural Organization, *Global Media and Information Literacy Assessment Framework: Country Readiness and Competencies*, Paris, 2013. As of April 24, 2019: http://unesdoc.unesco.org/images/0022/002246/224655e.pdf

University of Louisville, "Online Learning Modules," webpage, undated. As of April 23, 2019: https://library.louisville.edu/ekstrom/modules

University of Rhode Island, "Certificate of Graduate Study in Digital Literacy," webpage, undated. As of April 23, 2019: https://web.uri.edu/prov/certificate-credit-and-non-credit-program/digitalliteracy/

Van Deursen, Alexander, and Jan Van Dijk, "Internet Skills and the Digital Divide," *New Media and Society*, Vol. 13, No. 6, 2011, pp. 893–911.

Van Deursen, Alexander, Ellen Johanna Helsper, and Rebecca Eynon, *Measuring Digital Skills: From Digital Skills to Tangible Outcomes Project Report*, London: London School of Economics, University of Twente, and Oxford Internet Institute, 2014.

Vraga, Emily K., and Melissa Tully, "Media Literacy Messages and Hostile Media Perceptions: Processing of Nonpartisan Versus Partisan Political Information," *Mass Communication and Society*, Vol. 18, No. 4, 2015, pp. 422–448.

Vraga, Emily K., Melissa Tully, Heather Akin, and Hernando Rojas, "Modifying Perceptions of Hostility and Credibility of News Coverage of an Environmental Controversy Through Media Literacy," *Journalism: Theory, Practice and Criticism*, Vol. 13, No. 7, 2012, pp. 942–959.

Vraga, Emily K., Melissa Tully, and Hernando Rojas, "Media Literacy Training Reduces Perception of Bias," *Newspaper Research Journal*, Vol. 30, No. 4, 2009, pp. 68–81.

Warner, Dorothy Anne, "Programmatic Assessment: Turning Process into Practice by Teaching for Learning," *Journal of Academic Librarianship*, Vol. 29, No. 3, 2003, pp. 169–176.

Wineburg, Sam, Sarah McGrew, Joel Breakstone, and Teresa Ortega, *Evaluating Information: The Cornerstone of Civic Online Reasoning*, Stanford, Calif.: Stanford Digital Repository, Stanford University, 2016.

About the Authors

Alice Huguet is an associate policy researcher at the RAND Corporation. She is interested in educational policies that have the potential to influence the academic and life opportunities of students attending urban schools. She employs qualitative methods to better understand complex environmental, institutional, and organizational factors that intersect with the design and implementation of such policies. Huguet's research explores a variety of topics, including evidence-based decision-making at the district, school, and classroom levels; school leadership; interorganizational relationships; social and emotional learning; and alternative teacher preparation programs.

Jennifer Kavanagh is a senior political scientist at the RAND Corporation and associate director of the Strategy, Doctrine, and Resources Program in the RAND Arroyo Center. Her research focuses on U.S. political institutions and public opinion and their implications for U.S. foreign and domestic policy. Her work with RAND's President and CEO, Michael Rich, defines Truth Decay as the diminishing reliance on facts and data in U.S. political and civil discourse and describes its causes and consequences.

Garrett Baker is a policy analyst at the RAND Corporation. His work spans a variety of topics, including measurement of noncognitive skills, youth sports participation and funding, community violence, and technology in jails.

Marjory S. Blumenthal is a senior policy researcher at the RAND Corporation. Previously, she ran the President's Council of Advisors on Science and Technology at the White House Office of Science and Technology Policy, and before that she was associate provost, academic, at Georgetown University, developing academic strategy, strengthening the sciences and the overall research program, and promoting innovation in areas from international engagement to teaching and learning Before starting at Georgetown, Blumenthal was the founding executive director of the National Academies' Computer Science and Telecommunications Board. At RAND, Blumenthal has been working on assessing research, citizen science, technology and the future of cities, wireless communication, regulatory policy, and artificial intelligence, among other things.